THE BILLY REDMAYNE MEMORIAL FUND

FORWORD

I have no idea when I started to think about telling Billy's short but action-packed life story, but it was probably down to chatting to people a good while after the accident, and the comedy of errors that occurred in the 25 days we had to wait to have his funeral.

So here I go moving forward and closing one door.

In April 2022 it will be six years since Billy died. Six years seems like yesterday to me, yep that old cliché but it does. I can smell and feel him, I can hear the ventilator so clear that it seems like yesterday not 2,190 days which it will be on the 17th of April 2022.

So, I decided to tell our story warts and all - the journey we are still on and always will be the story of an ordinary family (some may want to question this).

Billy was born on the 6th of February 1991 in Accrington Lancashire, it was a Wednesday much to the delight of his dad Dave as this was the day the Motorcycle News came out, so whilst I did all the hard work Dave read the MCN which he had brought along with him and devoured a bacon bap. Dave still has that copy today.

It was 4 weeks later Billy's life hung in the balance, he had contracted a form of meningitis, the doctors said if he made it through the next 24 hours, he would be fine, nobody could prepare you for the fact that 24 hours feels like a week in those circumstances. Billy won his battle, but little did we know he had 2 more battles to fight in the next few years, one of which he would not win.

We got the phone call on Sunday the 17th of April; I have no idea what the time was. We then realised we faced the impossible situation of not being able to get off the island as there are no boats; the airport is shut so no planes and your loved one is seriously injured on life support; the decisions you must make quickly and knowing your world will never be whole again; living day to day with a big ache in your tummy.

I don't know what I expected of an ICU ward but certainly not what I experienced. I know each person will have their own opinions, but this is my experience and how I wish I had more colourful memories.

I can't go back and change what those dark days were like, I can't even remember how many days we were there. I am not criticising the ward at all the staff were awesome as you will find out later, what I am hoping to do is help other families.

We were very lucky to have the support of the parachute regiment and the special forces support group (SFSG), without them I don't think we would have got the answers we wanted.

The hospital was good, but what I found difficult was that the lack of information was a big deal. Who do we speak to? What do we do? Where do we stay? How much is it going to cost? The army did this for us. It still affects me to this day what would we have done if he hadn't been in the army?

I began to think, if I write about our journey maybe it will get out there and other families can look back at the silly things you do, say, and think. Or some people you thought where good friends don't get in touch anymore Yep that's quite normal. It's also about motor cycling being brilliant and gaining another family that, will always remember your loved one and the achievements they made on and off the bike it's also about the club you end up in but don't want to be in.

So, write your thoughts and silly memories them down, put them in your phone, take photos, yes take photos. Death is very rarely spoken about, let alone laughed about. I am not saying it will work for everyone but if you picked this book up, you must be curious and likeminded. It's about trying to change the way we think about death, especially in the young if it's a tragic accident or unexpected death. To me it was about keeping Billy's sense of humour going and what he would have done or said if the roles were reversed. I like to think he's looking down laughing his silly laugh, saying give it a go mum you have nowt to lose.

Bushy's 1994

Eden Camp 1999

Ripon 1999

CHAPTER ONE
"An obstacle is often a steppingstone" (Prescott)

Billy was your normal little boy. He had two older sisters, Kerry and Leanne, who he had a bit of a love/hate relationship with. We moved to the island when Billy was one, and his sisters were both at primary school. We had been on holiday previously for the Manx Grand Prix and fell in love with the place. Dave had been many times before with the lads.

We rented a house in Onchan which had a concrete back garden. I cannot remember how many times I took Billy to Noble's Hospital in the six months we were there; every single one was for a knock on the head - nothing changes - but it was enough for them to question me about it.

Back garden in Onchan 1992

The first one was in the school holidays, it was a big fall followed by not a lot of crying, hmm, this was a worry. I got the kids in the car and headed off to where I thought the hospital was. I saw a sign saying, 'Nobles Hospital', but pointing to a one-way street (I now know this is standard), so I pulled up to ask a lady. By this time, I had one screaming son, daughter number 2 Leanne crying because Billy was crying and daughter number 1 Kerry shouting to calm them down. I asked the lady the way to KNOBLYS Hospital. Well, the girls started laughing and the lady, bless her, told me how it was pronounced, and I drove away very red-faced, but glad I didn't know anybody over here. Billy and the girls were all laughing as we entered casualty, typical.

Billy went to nursery from the age of 18 months. He enjoyed going and mixed well with the other children.

He loved cycling from an early age, he was very competitive even then. At 3 years old he went cycling at the Criterium League races (now called Manx Youth Races) at the National Sports Centre in Douglas, run by the lovely Dot Tilbury. She still runs it today. He was about 5 years old and had won a trophy. He had to go on stage to collect it, and as he walked on Dot said, 'Here's Billy Redmayne, another Joey Dunlop in the making'. He was well chuffed.

Ramsey promenade 1995

Billy also enjoyed a kick-about after school with his friends and calling for his friend down the road called Andrew. When no one else was out, he used to take his dog, Rob, and put him in goal. He was actually a very intelligent border collie.

He went to Ashley Hill primary school in Onchan and played football for them, as well as Laxey AFC. He was probably around 7 years old at this point. He later switched and played for Corinthians, where most of his mates went. He got on well with his coach Billy Crowe at Corinthians. Whilst playing for them he won a few trophies and the team won the Junior FA cup out at St Johns on a very rare hot sunny day, which made a welcome change from the usual wet windy ones.

The report Billy achieved on leaving Ashley Hill school from the headmaster, Mr Huntley, was a very good one, which said Billy will be 'a leader of men', which I thought was very strange for an 11-year old's report, but hey-ho.

By the age of 11/12, Billy was picked to train with the Isle of Man FA School of Excellence, and later represented the Isle of Man against the Everton Juniors. He was impressed that he could play for the Isle of Man or England - as he was born in Lancashire, he had dual nationality.

Whilst Billy was at Park Road school for years 7 & 8, he told us tales of getting paid for going to the shops for other pupils due to him having a dinner pass off us, creative little sod. Despite this, I received a telephone call from school saying we should be very proud of Billy as he had stopped a fight at lunch time, where a few boys where picking on a younger coloured boy. Good one, Billy. In the meantime, we thought he was doing well and enjoying himself with his football, but no, he decided he was never going to be professional footballer and that was that. No changing his mind or any encouragement worked, so here we go on Billy's next adrenalin fix.

He wanted to go out doing jumps on his push bike with his mates in Douglas. Fair enough, it was free! Apart from the 'Mum I'm late, can you run me to the grandstand? and luckily, we had a van, and the bike would fit in. 'We will help all we can,' - he kept reminding me that I had said that when we moved to Laxey, and it would bite me in the arse for a long time. He once showed us some footage on his phone of him having a massive crash - wow, there was many more to come, he was quite impressed by it! Me, not so much.

Then came the next level, motorbikes, but we couldn't come up with the parents' speech of 'they are too dangerous', as

Dave and I both had bikes and he had been on the back of mine since he was 3 years old, going to nursery! I had told him he could go on the back with me, like his sisters did, when his feet could touch the foot pegs.

I came out of the house one morning a few months later to find Billy ready with his bag and wellies on, saying his feet could touch the pegs now. I sat him on the back and fair enough, they did. We arrived at nursery after a short ride and as I went to help him off, he jumped and shrank; his feet were not in his wellies properly, but the wellies were on the foot pegs. This is the kind of determination and obstacles he overcame that got Billy to where he wanted to go in life!

We then got him a second hand DT125, which I occasionally used to go to work on in the evenings - much to his annoyance. He enjoyed riding around fields on it and learnt to ride it very quickly. One “off” was at Dowty’s field in Onchan, which resulted in a broken arm, and the first of many trips to Noble’s hospital.

Garage at Laxey 2005 (DT125 in the background)

The hardest thing to sort out for off-road practicing is somewhere to do it, and I have to say, for an island predominantly known for motorcycling both on and off road, there are very few places for people to practice riding safely.

Due to Dave and I never having enough spare time together, Billy was lucky to have both parents to take him out practicing, to Foxdale Dead's, Snuff the Wind, or Sky Hill in Ramsey. His dad took him at weekends, and I took him out in the evenings or school holidays. Billy also enjoyed going to the Youth Motor Project funded by the Board of Education, run by a lovely man, Pete Hodgson, whom Billy had a lot of respect for.

One weekend whilst out on the bike at Foxdale, someone who was also out riding said Billy was ready for the Moto X track. Once again Dave and I discussed it, as this would mean a different bike, so we agreed that Billy would have to pull his finger out and do jobs at home, as I had to do extra shifts at work to cover the bike, body armour, new boots, fuel and anything else! Billy agreed to do anything, including walking the dogs and emptying the dishwasher. He also had to be nice to his sisters, as he would need marshals at every meeting.

We bought him a Yamaha YZ 85 as a surprise for him. We bought it in October 2004, put it in the garage and trimmed it up as it was his Christmas present, but early, so he could fit a couple of rounds in at Knock Froy and Ballagaraghan Moto X tracks. We all enjoyed, or should I say endured, the weekends spent supporting him.

Every Moto X track I have ever marshalled at has been very windy and near the coast. Why? So, you end up with windburn, and numb hands and feet. When he was representing the Isle of Man at a place called Haverigg in Cumbria on his YZ 125, as he had outgrown the 85cc bike, I got bitten by a horsefly and ended up in the ambulance being treated, and it was constantly repeated over the tannoy, so I am told, that leaving my marshals post unmanned, despite feeling quite ill, nearly got Billy disqualified - eeek. The Island team didn't win, but we all had a good time and some of us had family come to visit which was nice.

Haverigg, Cumbria 2006

It was around this time that we started fostering. The girls had left home, and we had moved to a new house, from Onchan to a cottage next to the Laxey wheel. I had looked after Adam, the little boy we fostered, for a few years at work. The whole family got on with him and he fitted in very well as he liked football, bikes, and army films.

Billy and Adam got on very well, like brothers. There were quite a few times I caught Billy making Adam jump whilst feeding our five dogs, by shooting at him with his BB gun, but making sure he hit the tin dishes to maximise the noise. Adam took it all in good humour. He also enjoyed a kick about and showing Adam what to do with the bike in the garage and quite often managed to "persuade" Adam to wash it after a motocross event. He said it was teaching him skills.

Billy and Adam

Billy then decided he needed a new motorbike. We bought it for him, and Billy paid us back. He had a job after school at Manx Engineers two minutes from our house. Lucky Billy. It is now Ballacregga Cornmill Cafe. He needed the new bike, because at 15 you could ride a 250cc in the adult class at Moto X.

Chapter 2
"Accept the challenges so that you may feel the exhilaration of victory" (David Salton)

When the time came for Billy to leave school in June 2007, he had a few weeks spare before he could start his job as an electrician's mate at the new prison that was being built at Jurby. He wanted money as it was TT fortnight, so I asked him to chop some bushes down in the garden. He moaned but did it. The next day was Sunday, a MotoX Day, but Billy refused to get up. Not like him when bikes are involved. Dad went back up to check on him and discovered big red marks up his arms. Billy was very delirious, so off to Noble's again - this time for blood poisoning from the bloody trees because he didn't wear the gloves, I gave him.

The Poisonous Tree Laxey

After 24 hours he was looking and feeling better. He was very lucky as we managed to catch it early before it spread, but he was not allowed home as he needed monitoring. Billy said he felt a fraud, even though he was on a drip for four days, as Barry Wood was in the next bed, head to toe in bandages. He had crashed at Tower Bends during practice.

Billy was hoping to get in the army, something he had wanted since he was very young. It was the one thing that had not changed. After working in the prison for a while, he said he could never work in the same place every day for the rest of his working life; the only fun he was having was the ride to and from work on the trusty DT125.

Luckily for him he signed his allegiance for the army on 12th December 2007. It was a proud day for all of us. He left home to join up in January 2008 to go to Harrogate Army Foundation College. We took him across and left him in the safe hands of the British Army. He rang often and was encouraged to write letters home, which are nice to have now.

He found it hard at the beginning as he couldn't march and had to do extra drills to get it right. He had leave after six weeks and was a different person than the one we dropped off. He could iron and keep his room clean, and he could also eat a damn sight more!
But there was more to him as a person; he would offer to make lunch for both of us if he was at home during the day, and one day I was painting the ceiling in the kitchen when I

suddenly remembered I had to be at a meeting for our foster child, and Billy said, 'Don't panic, I will iron your pants whilst you have a shower'.

Heck, if that's what the army does, brilliant. I did get the odd reminders when he wanted a lift anywhere: 'Remember mum, I did iron your pants so pleeease run me, I am not being a bus wanker.

The sooner he learned to drive the better it would be, all round. A few weeks later he passed his test. Yeah, we didn't need to run him anywhere, and better still, he could drop us at the pub and pick us up. Win-win. He just needed a vehicle.

In a couple of weeks' time, he would be going to Catterick Garrison to do P company which is a 28-week intense training course testing physical and mental endurance. In test week you have eight tests:

1. A 10-miler carrying a 35lb Bergen rucksack and rifle, to be completed in 1 hour 50 minutes or under.
2. Trainasium - an assault course designed to test a candidate's head for heights.
3. Log race – an 8-man team carrying 60kg over 1.9km.
4. 2-mile march, carrying 35lb Bergen, food, water and a rifle, to be completed in 18 minutes or under.
5. Steeplechase - a 1.8mile cross country course featuring water obstacles and an assault course.
6. Milling - milling tests whether the recruit has the aggression and determination required of a Paratrooper.

Recruits must aggressively pummel their opponent whilst wearing boxing gloves and headguard.

7. Endurance March - 20 miles carrying 35lb Bergen with water, food and a rifle, to be completed in 4 hours or under.
8. Stretcher Race – 16-man teams carrying a175lb stretcher over 5 miles.

On completion of PPS Pre-Parachute Selection, a recruit is eligible to wear the coveted maroon beret and can move on to parachute training.

Once again, he had our full support. He passed and sent us a text message which read, "passed 1 para-A coy". I was so proud that I cried, from relief I think, as he would have been unbearable had he failed.

Dave & Billy Catterick passing out 2009

Sue & Billy Catterick passing out 2009

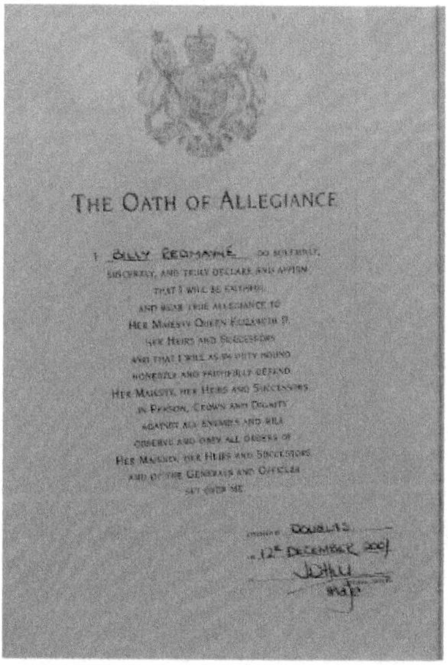

THE OATH OF ALLEGIANCE

I BILLY REDMAYNE DO SOLEMNLY,
SINCERELY, AND TRULY DECLARE AND AFFIRM
THAT I WILL BE FAITHFUL
AND BEAR TRUE ALLEGIANCE TO
HER MAJESTY QUEEN ELIZABETH II,
HER HEIRS AND SUCCESSORS
AND THAT I WILL AS IN DUTY BOUND
HONESTLY AND FAITHFULLY DEFEND
HER MAJESTY, HER HEIRS AND SUCCESSORS
IN PERSON, CROWN AND DIGNITY
AGAINST ALL ENEMIES AND WILL
OBSERVE AND OBEY ALL ORDERS OF
HER MAJESTY, HER HEIRS AND SUCCESSORS
AND OF THE GENERALS AND OFFICERS
SET OVER ME

[illegible] DOUGLAS
12th DECEMBER 200[illegible]

Chapter 3
"One who smiles rather than angers is always stronger" (Chinese proverb)

In early November 2010, aged just 19, he was getting ready for his first tour of Afghanistan He got up (very surprisingly before dinner) and asked if I fancied a McDonald's. Yep! So, I drove, and he paid but it took us an age as we got the giggles when I tried to order at the drive-through.

Billy always called the Chicken Legend Meal a 'leg end' so, as I got to the drive through window, I ended up saying 'Two leg end meals please'. We couldn't stop laughing, so I had to abandon the order until we calmed down and then I went in and ordered it, I still laugh at that today. It's the little memories that keep you going or crack you up.

Later, he wanted an afternoon out with his mates, Nikki and Joey so I let him borrow my L200 pick-up truck. He was insured, what could happen? I said he could but had to pick our foster child Tom up from school. Yes, no problem.

Then I got a phone call: "Mum, I have banged the truck". Oh heck, I said, can you still collect Tom for me? "No mum, it's a big bang, I don't think it will mend." I asked if everyone was okay and he said yes, police were on their way, so I rang his dad and explained what had happened. Dave went to Peel, which was the other end of the island from where he was working, to pick up Billy and his mates.

The Dead L200 Peel to Kirk Michael coast road

When he arrived, Billy was talking to a policeman who was ex-military and understood the hassle it would cause Billy, seeing as he was off to foreign parts soon. Very lucky for Billy. Kerry luckily finished at 3pm so she could collect Tom. I did often think to myself why he didn't stick to football, much calmer and safer, then I tell myself, and boring.

Drama over, except for Billy's debrief of the crash, which goes like this: "But Dad, honestly, I wasn't going that fast, the back end just stepped out and I thought I had saved it, but it just shot into the wall. As both airbags deployed there was a familiar smell of cordite and the front of the stereo hit my nose and Alvin the chipmunk despatched himself through the window, but it was okay as I found him in the grass later." Billy thought coming home with my Alvin, but no vehicle was fine!

Meanwhile, back in the normal world, friends Phil, Marie and Wayne Danby who ran the local pub, The Bridge Inn in Laxey, organised a party for Billy which was an awesome send off for him, despite writing off my prize truck.

The Bridge Hotel Laxey

I was proud of him, but still a scared mum. I had nightmares that he would be captured by the Taliban, and they would torture him. They were hideous, and very vivid.

Dave tried to reassure me (whether that was just so that he could get back to sleep), saying that Billy was safer than a lot of soldiers out there as he was Special Forces Support Group (SFSG), attached to the SAS. It helped me a little bit, but I wasn't convinced. I told Billy I understood how exciting it was for him. With all the training they had done, to not go and fight would be like training for a race you were never going to do. But I was still scared for him.

Oman 2010

One thing I always do when I want to know about something is buy a book, none of this internet stuff. This time I went for a book called Daffodil Girls by Kitty Dimbleby, short stories of love, loss and friendship by the people behind the heroes of war.

It made me realise I was not the only mum feeling like this; scared, proud, knots in your tummy trying to be brave basically the fear of the unknown. Along with Billy going to a war zone, our daughter Kerry was going travelling on her own, meeting up with friends in Australia and New Zealand, plus other exotic places like Thailand, Cambodia, Vietnam and China. Leanne, our other daughter, lived in York so I couldn't even meet up with her for coffee and chat. It was just me and Dave.

We decided to go away until Billy landed in Afghanistan. I couldn't just sit at home worrying about things we couldn't control, even though I knew he would be back for R&R (rest and recuperation) in a few months.

Christmas Afghanistan 2010

We went to Belfast for a few days and had a brilliant time. The Christmas markets were on. We got chatting to a chap from the Royal Irish Regiment who had served under captain Doug Beattie in Afghanistan. Dave had just read Beattie's book 'An Ordinary Soldier'! Weird world. He did put our minds at rest a little, and was a lovely chap.

Then when we got home the worrying started. I had decided to keep my mind off "the situation in Afghanistan" which seemed to be the opening words on the news every hour, along with the bloody earthquake in New Zealand and bushfires in Australia. Hell, these kids are putting us through it! I needed to do something to keep my mind occupied, something positive. We had three border collies, so the obvious thing to do was run, and so that I couldn't chicken out I got everyone in the local pubs to sponsor me. I ran to raise money for Help for Heroes. It kept me focused.

We knew all the training the lads had done. Billy told us as much as he was allowed, they had done pre-deployment training in Oman. We knew he was out there doing night operations, and as a mum I was scared for him being in the dark, not that I would let him know. He rang as often as he could, but it was quite often a one-sided conversation as the satellite phone calls were monitored.

Pre-deployment training Oman

Being a Goon Afghanistan

I can remember quite often in the early days of Billy's deployment I would freak out when the phone rang. I would run upstairs and tell Dave to get it. Dave always said it's the door you need to worry about, if anything happens, they won't ring us, they will send somebody. I still wasn't convinced.

Billy managed to ring home a few times. One conversation that still makes me giggle was Billy telling me he had been on the night shift, and before sleeping they went to the gym. A cat kept going in, so they fed it. I asked what they had called it, he replied 'Nowt'.

I laughed and said what a brilliant name for a cat, to which he replied, 'Oh mother, we haven't named it!' 'Oh, ha, it is a good name, do you want me to send any food for it?' 'No ta mum. This place is massive, double the size of Blackburn, I could buy a car if I wanted, the Yanks have everything.' I remember saying to him, 'Tom would love him to buy an American car like the one in the Dukes of Hazzard.'

"Nowt" the cat Afghanistan

Funny the snippets of conversation stay with you. He also rang to say thanks for his treat parcels, a little bit of home in a box. He also asked for sweets for the Afghan children. It seemed alien going to the supermarket for things like that with your everyday shopping, wondering what the children would like to eat or what their ages were.

Chapter 4
"The hard way is the right way" (John Alves)

The tour went slowly for us. Billy had lost friends out there prior to being deployed, and others had been injured. It brought it closer to home for us all. One friend Billy talked about was a lad from 2 Para called Martin Bell. Billy quite often told us about the antics they got up to. One of many that sticks in my mind (that is printable!) was one evening when the lads were bored and skint, so they had a few drinks at camp and headed out. Bell had heard of a party going on. I don't know how, but they managed to get invited in. Billy said they each said they knew someone there and they managed to get fed, drunk, and ended up spooning in a single bed. Well done lads, it's far better than the Biffa bins, which I will come to later.

Martin was deployed in October 2010. He was serving with 2 Para, and whilst on duty he risked his life in a minefield to rescue a wounded comrade. Martin, 24, was killed after giving lifesaving first aid to a soldier who had lost both his legs, after stepping on an improvised explosive device. Martin from Bradford was given the George Medal posthumously. I never got to meet Martin, but wish I had.

Night out with Martin Bell

Billy came back from his tour in January for R&R physically unharmed, but I think he was a little bit mentally scarred. Who wouldn't be after being out there for three months and knowing you had to go back for another three?

Billy flew to Brize Norton and got the train to his sister's house in York. Dave and I arrived from the island with the van the next day. Billy looked tired.

I was so overwhelmed I could hardly speak. I gave him his usual mum hug – God, it felt good. Leanne told us that Billy had slept a lot and talked a lot, which we were happy about. We all went out for a bite to eat and drinks, which must have seemed a bit weird for Billy.

Later that evening Billy talked of Bell and other friends and family he had lost, and Dave and I just sat listened. To be honest, for such a young age Billy had lost both his great grandparents, three grandparents and three friends, not including those whom he lost from the Paras, so a few beers (out, out!!!) and lots of talking helped him, which I am so grateful for. The outcome could have been worse had he not talked about it.

We returned to the island the following day. Billy spent a lot of his leave sleeping. To be fair, it was nice listening to his snoring, and he could snore! I did have to pull him up a few times - he would often ask if I wanted a brew, usually when I was cleaning the chickens out at the bottom of the garden, and a while later I would walk up to the kitchen looking for my brew and Billy would say 'Bloody hell mum, you drank it, do you not remember? The so-and-so had forgot to make it, and he got me with this on almost every leave. He made me think I was losing my mind.

Whilst he was away, Billy asked his dad to put a deposit on an old ambulance for him, which he was going to use as his race bus. When the lads go off on tour, they get an ops bonus, and Billy was using some of this.

Billy and I went out to collect it, which again just had us in fits of laughter as the lights and Nee-NAWS still worked. He looked so out of place driving an ambulance with his stupid grin.

Dave and I had already collected his new race bike for him. It was a 2005 CBR600. He was hoping to do a track day whilst on leave, but the weather was not good enough. I just wanted a calm normal day - sod the adrenalin fix, let's just chill.

Jurby Race Track Isle of Man 2011

Later Billy decided to use his old ZXR600 in part exchange for a lovely black R6 to use instead of his broken ZXR, getting the train, or using my Suzuki 600 Bandit to get to the ferry and leaving her on the high street in Catterick when he came home. I went up to the garage to have a look and sat on it. It was lovely, yep - mum was jealous, I could touch the floor and she looked sexy! (The bike not me).

I promised Bill I would try and have his race bus finished and looking good by the time his tour finished in May 2011, plus it was his birthday present. We were lucky enough to have Billy him home for his 20th birthday on 6th February. As mentioned earlier, we were fostering a young boy called Tom, and lucky for Billy, Tom loved vehicles of all shapes and sizes - basically anything with wheels. He still does. Tom really went to town with me trying to get all the stickers off. Adam came to help it was a family job, but hard work - have you ever tried to get stickers off an ambulance mixed with paint stripper? It represents sticky snot, yuk.

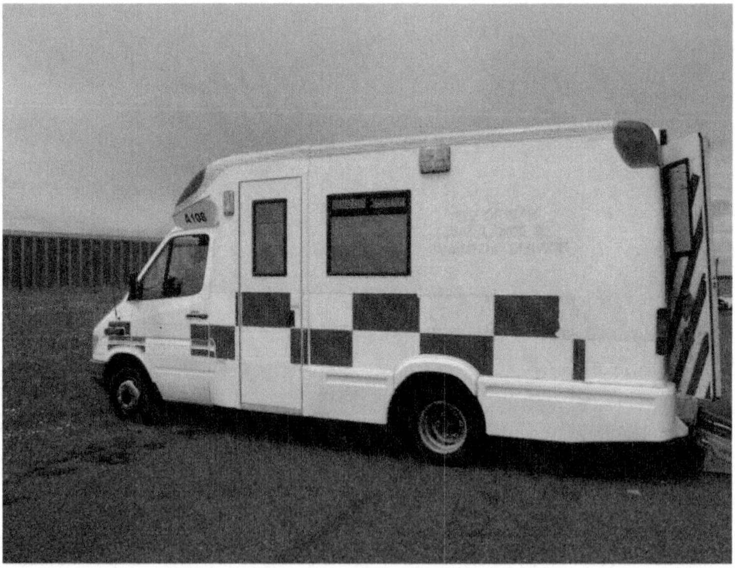

Race bus (The Ambo)

He was due home the beginning of June. He would be getting off the ferry at 6.30am and coming through Laxey village. I asked Phil at the Bridge Pub if I could put a welcome banner and flags out so that Billy would see them when he came through. He helped Tom and I put them up.

June 2011 "mums soldiers' home"

The Bridge Pub, Laxey.

Well, I thought he will either laugh at it or be furious - either way it's done now. He said he was surprised and had a chuckle, 'Welcome Home Billy', and lots of bunting outside our cottage. I had put 'Mum's Soldier is Home'. I was so excited I didn't really care. He would be home and safe soon. Billy enjoyed his time off, once he had slept a lot and readjusted. By this time, he was the best poached egg maker going (his words), but to be fair, they were good, along with his tuna cheese melts.

He enjoyed meeting up with his friends Nikki, Joey, Jim, Gaz, and others too numerous to mention, sorry. He took me out on the back of the R6 to collect my new truck that had had a tyre fitted. I swore blind I would never get on the back of him again. I am sure Nikki said something similar after a trip over the mountain.
He was lucky enough to be able to race his 2005 Honda at Jurby in June and July. In August good friends of ours offered Billy a lift for him and his bike plus a bed in the father Fagan race bus, to race at Anglesey. Brilliant opportunity for him.

2011 a wet Anglesey

Father Fagan was a side car racer at the time and is a lovely man. He is also an ordained priest, why? Dave, me and Tom

decided we would go and have a bit of a holiday and give Tom a chance to explore another island. We had a brilliant time, despite being wet and windy, and according to Father Fagan my son 'purrs, not snores'.

Billy got a 1st, and if I remember, it was in the wet. Nerve-wracking for me. Why do dads stand there so proud, but mums feel proud but can't watch? That was my first of many trips away to watch him on the circuit instead of a muddy track.

We had a few trips away to various race meetings with good friends and meeting up with family. Billy returned to camp (work). We didn't see a lot of Billy in 2011. We did hear a lot about him though.

Chapter 5
"Fall seven times stand up eight".
(Japanese proverb)

In August, Billy and a few paras who had finished their first tour went off to Ibiza for a holiday. Unbeknownst to Billy, his dad and I had seen something on TV about paras in Ibiza dressed in togas invading night clubs, so we had a rough idea what he would be up to. Billy told Kerry that they played Swedish House Mafia's 'Antidote' on full blast very early in the morning, regardless of the time you hit your pit. I feel for anyone trying to have a nice break at that time. It is a lovely island, we have been once, and I would go back.

Ibiza 2011

Billy returned home in February for his 21st birthday which was on the 6th. He went out on the Saturday with friends, and on the Sunday the 5th he was godfather to Leo Gray.

How he managed to get booted and suited and there on time is a miracle, called dad.

Billy with Leo

Leo with Billy

Billy was lucky enough to have a few weekends free to race. He went to Oulton Park with his dad in April 2012, again with his trusty Honda 2005 CBR600. Then in May he managed to fit Jurby in before heading back to Afghanistan on Operation Rego.

When, I look back now, my life was just a complete whirlwind of tours and race circuits. Everything seemed to be done at 100 miles an hour. This time when he went back, I knew it was a short tour, so I decided to keep busy. I would run every day, be it one mile or ten, rain or shine. I did regret it some days but told myself the lads out there were going through 10 times more shit, so I carried on.

We continued to send parcels out to Billy, Irish Road Racer magazine being one request, and some decent whisky. How was I supposed to do that? Apparently other mums did, so please could I, 'I am sure you will find a way mum'. Well, I did, and sent some out numerous times, along with sweets for the Afghan children.

Billy came back from his tour one evening - I was sat in my PJs trying to catch up with some me-time with the TV when the phone rang - is it just mothers that know? Here we go, I thought. Dave answered. Yep, it was Billy, he had crashed his R6 at the Gooseneck. That roughly translates to “Help mum, dad, I’ve wrote it off and hurt myself, get me to the hospital before the police come”.

Oh no the broken R6!

Dave went off to the Gooseneck in the ambulance. He then rang me; Billy had hurt his foot. I sat their cursing Billy and motorcycles. Then I got a phone call from Billy; could I collect him please from Nobles Hospital. He had broken two toes. Dave had put the bike in the ambulance and Billy was stuck on crutches with no lift home. "Yes darling, no problem, I will just put my wine back and get out of my PJs." Argh!

I collected him, helped him in the vehicle and made him comfy. He then said, 'I am starving mum, can you get me a Chinese?"
This injury he got would come back to bite him later. I didn't laugh much when it did. We also got to watch the crash - he had it on his GoPro - not nice, but at least we could see where he went wrong. Despite his crash and writing the R6 off, he was able to do a track day at Cadwell Park in September. This is where his injury from the R6 crash comes back to bite him. We all went to the ferry in the race bus (ambo). Dave's Firestorm was in the back, as after the track day Dave and I were going to meet friends at Oliver's Mount for the Gold Cup. We were staying in a pub in Louth. We had a meal, a few beers and a chat. Billy said his foot was aching - he had jumped off a rock on tour and hurt the same foot as before, but nothing to worry about.

Billy resting his 'soapy' foot Cadwell 2012.

Dave and I went up to a comfy bed and Billy slept in the ambo with the bike in the car park, in a not-so-comfy bed. Next morning after Billy's sneaky shower, they set off to the racetrack.

I did some shopping and our daughter Leanne, who lived in York, picked me up and off we went to Cadwell. At least the sun was shining. As we got there, we could tell by their faces there was a problem. Billy couldn't get his boot on his foot which had swollen, probably from the drive up. I went back to the hotel, and we used shower gel, shampoo, anything to squeeze his foot in his boots. He was in agony but managed to get a good track session in.

In 2013 Billy was able to complete a full season with Derby Phoenix. He now had a 2010 Honda CBR 600rr. He did most of the season on his own, but still finished 8th overall.

I remember one-time Dave and I decided to surprise him at Aintree. We got the ferry over and I rang him as we were docking and told him to put the kettle on, we would be there soon. He was very surprised to say the least, and eager for help and advice of his dad.
It was this day that we met Ringo, who was helping Billy. He was a medic based at the same camp as Billy, and a keen biker. He would go on to be a good friend of ours to this day.

Chapter 6
"Out of difficulties grow miracles".
(Jean De Le Bruyere)

In May 2014 we met Billy's girlfriend. She had driven to Cadwell Park to watch Billy race. In Billy's usual way he said, "Mum, can you drive down and meet Hannah at the gate? She's got blonde hair!" I found her, as there weren't that many people around. I introduced myself and off we went - talk about awkward and embarrassing, but I'm sure Hannah will say the same, but we got on okay. We went over to watch his race together and he got two wins and two seconds.

Billy jumping The Mountain at Cadwell

Billy then went back out to Afghanistan in June to work as part of Tiger Teams, teaching Afghanistan soldiers to fight against the Taliban. In order to do this, he had to learn to speak Pashto, which he did. Proud Mama moment there. It was on this tour that he got me a lovely Afghan rug! He told me he asked one of the Afghan soldiers to find one for him. Bless him, it wasn't like he was on holiday, and I was only joking when I said he was in the right place to bring me a genuine Afghan rug back.

Mums Afghan rug

Next on the agenda was Billy doing the Manx Grand Prix whilst home on his on his R&R. Oh okay. Dave had the task of sorting the bike for him, which he did enjoy doing, in our little cramped garage in Laxey. Billy arrived home in August with just enough time to do the Newcomers laps, plus a few laps in my "new" truck. He had watched a lot of YouTube laps whilst not on duty.

Again, I was asked to go and meet someone I didn't know, Ian – "He's in a van and has a dog." Okay, off I went to meet Ian. He spotted me first and followed me up to the paddock. It was here I believe that Ian met our friend Rhys Hardisty, his girlfriend Becky and mum Maria for the first time. They discovered they didn't live that far away from each other. It's a small world.

We had it tough in a paddock farthest away from the grandstand and only the ambo and Ian's van to use. As we were locals, we were in the day paddock, but the weather was kind, so we all managed. Ian and Billy spent many a night after practice in the garage. Dave was scrutineering till late, then going into the garage, and having debriefs, watching the onboard laps he had done. I just continued to cook and feed people at random times, plus I helped with Charly, Ian`s dog, who was good company as all of mine were in kennels. The lads seemed to have it all sorted for the races: Ian was mechanic, Jim visor man, Mally fuel man. They had practiced pit stops on the Laxey fire station car park!

Father Fagan had sponsored Billy for two races, which funnily enough turned out to be £666. He had sponsors from a lot of people which I know he was surprised at and grateful for. I will mention them all at the end of the book. I was very lucky to have Rhys mum, Maria, to talk to and worry with, as Rhys was out there racing as well, and in 1998 Maria lost her husband Ian Charles Hardisty at the TT in the Production Race. They home stayed with us and Billy and Rhys who were 7 and 10 at the time shared a room and enjoyed playing imaginary motor cross bikes together.

I told Billy on the morning of the Newcomers Race that I would watch with the girls and our friends, Steg and Lung, at the Gooseneck. I like it there as you can hear them at Schoolhouse in Ramsey, then Parliament Square, up to the Hairpin and round Tower Bends. It sounds awesome, especially if there's a few, plus that's where he broke his R6.

Pit board at the Gooseneck MGP 14

The girls were pit-boarding for him, and his dad was scrutineering bikes for the racing, but not Billy's bike, so his dad was getting all the live timings on the computer screen.

Start line Newcomers Race, with Mally Oates & Jim Marshall 2014

I heard/saw Billy coming up the hill from Waterworks on his first lap. I was proud, excited, and felt sick. I closed my eyes. He was in the lead; I had another 3 laps to endure - eeek. I decided to watch from Hillberry, and I got there in time to see him go past on his third lap. He seemed to be going faster. It was between him and Malachi Mitchel Thomas. I couldn't stand it, I set off to the grandstand and again in good time to see him come in and win.

Winning the newcomers race 2014

That Smile

His smile said it all. I said, 'Did you enjoy that?' 'Yeah, mum I did', with a smile I will never forget. Then he promised me the Junior race would be more sedate, he had done what he came to do, so he was taking it steady. Yep okay, sure you will. He took it that steady he came 2nd and did the fastest lap of the race.

All I had to worry about now was him going back to finish his tour. I am not religious at all, but I did do some silent prayers to anyone who could hear me. We all went to the awards presentation later, all of us still on a high. It was at the grandstand in Douglas, and it was an evening I will never forget, I treasure it. Our friends came and the lads who had helped pit for Billy. Unfortunately, Ian and Pete had to leave before the awards, jobs to do. Kerry our daughter videoed it on her phone, and I'm so glad she did - I relive that moment often. We all went into town after for a few more drinks and this is where Billy and his dad got chatting to Martin Bullock about riding for him in next year's Manx Grand Prix.

Enjoying his win before flying back to 'That place'

Billy was flying back out in the morning to camp, then on to Brize Norton, and
then that dreaded place. It all seemed so surreal. How do you go back to normal everyday life? What is normal?

Whilst Billy was away, friends of ours in Australia, Allen and Beau, rang to see if Billy fancied a ride in New Zealand in the Suzuki TRI series which consists of two short circuits and a street circuit, and which is run on Boxing Day in Whanganui. When Billy next rang, his dad gave him the news. He was buzzing.

Beau looking serious in New Zealand

After a lot of hard work and phone calls by dad, and flights and insurances sorted with help from Michelle Haynes at the ACU, he was good to go. He then realised he had booked a short break with Hannah to Egypt. He had to do security briefing first due to the climate out there and was told to always hide tattoos. Billy had just started a lovely sleeve tattoo he had to wrap it in clingfilm for showers and hide it best he could.

He was coming home on leave for a few days before they went on holiday. He set me a task of finding him some flip flops and shorts in October on the island. Not a chance. I told him to buy some out there.

Hannah & Billy Egypt 2014

Enjoying time with Hannah in Egypt

They had a great relaxing holiday, which is just what he needed before flying out to New Zealand in a few weeks. He had his Ops bonus left so he could just about financially manage do it. I told him I was jealous, as that was one place I would love to go, and his grandad had never got there. He went out there with two mates, Lex and Ash, who would spanner for him. What a fantastic opportunity, New Zealand for Christmas in the sunshine, and racing on Boxing Day.

The borrowed bike

I remember him ringing me from the airport and me saying to him 'It would be my dream to go out there watching bike racing in the sun at Christmas'. He replied, 'Well do it then mum'. That started me thinking about next year. Billy had obviously had a brilliant time and met lots of nice helpful people: Flea and Julie Willacy who are organisers at the Whanganui circuit found them somewhere to stay and invited them to Christmas dinner. Guy Martin, who took Billy round the track for a recce as he had raced it before, Guy's dad, who went to the pub after the awards evening with the lads and made a memorable evening talking about 9/11 conspiracies! and Joe, Barb and Perry Lett. Billy's bike, a Suzuki GSXR 600 blew up, so they lent Billy a Honda CBR 600, which luckily, he was more at home with, as it was what he had won the Manx Grand Prix on.

OOPS Billy off Beau's bike at Manfeild.

All in all, a good time was had, lots of nice genuine people, lots of sightseeing, bungie jumping, riding the Luge track, and no doubt drinking done. I vowed we would be there next year.

Fun times with Guy Martin

Chapter 7
"Never let your memories be bigger than your dreams" (Doug Ivester)

Billy arrived back in the UK to a complete climate change, but in time to spend the New Year with Hannah in Guildford on a houseboat. Billy apparently brought the 2015 New Year in by wetting the bed and poor Hannah had to sleep on the floor. Is there only my son who did this on a regular basis? Sorry Billy.

Then sometime in February I got a phone call from Billy. He was in London with a mate and Billy was getting presented with an award. He didn't say what, except it was a posh do and he wanted to go on the p--s after, but had not been paid - can I lend him some money? Yes, no problem, Billy! Ill transfer it now.

Later we received pictures of what the do was like, and who was there. On his left was General Sir Mike Jackson who at the time was head of the British Army and to his right was the boss of Barclays Bank. Eeek - glad he knew his P's & Q's.
We later discovered it was at the Fishmongers Hall and he was being awarded the Fishmongers Company Trophy by Colonel Commandant Sir John Lorimer, which was awarded to the most outstanding Parachute Regiment soldier from all four Battalions.
He was awarded it in 2014, but due to commitments with his job and racing in New Zealand he didn't collect it until February 2015. Another proud mum moment, although we

had to look online for its meaning as I had asked the question, "What has our Billy got to do with fishing?"

Fishmongers Hall, "what's our Billy got to do with fishing"?

BILLY REDMAYNE

The Fishmongers' Trophy is an annual award for outstanding achievement, made to a member or former member of The Parachute Regiment by the Fishmongers' Company.

This Livery Company is one of the twelve great Livery Companies of the City of London and among the most ancient of the City Guilds. The Fishmongers' Company is officially affiliated to The Parachute Regiment and this prestigious award is selected annually by the Colonel Commandant of the Regiment.

As the then Colonel Commandant of The Parachute Regiment, I selected Billy to be awarded the Fishmongers' Trophy for 2014. It was not a difficult decision, because in the previous twelve months, Billy had encapsulated everything that we wanted in our young paratroopers: drive, physical fitness, mental robustness, technical expertise, enthusiasm, energy and ambition. His skill at and passion for road racing motorcycling was well documented even then; indeed, as a Regiment, we were particularly proud that his motorcycles always sported The Parachute Regiment cap badge.

But it was his military excellence, professionalism and attitude to soldiering and love for our Regiment that also struck me.

In May 2014, Billy deployed to Afghanistan as a member of the First Battalion, The Parachute Regiment. As a result of this deployment, he was not able to compete in the build-up races for the Isle of Man Grand Prix (MGP). Nonetheless, he managed to secure a place as a consequence of his previous results. He then timed his two-week Rest and Recuperation (R&R) period away from Afghanistan, so that he could compete in the Manx GP races in August 2014. He attended the Manx GP and won the Newcomers Race and came second in the Junior Race, beating numerous full time professional motorcyclists. This was particularly impressive when one considers that he was riding an older and less powerful motorbike, worth a fraction of the price of those of the other riders. His success in 2014 entitled him to compete in the Isle of Man Tourist Trophy (TT) the next year. At the 2014 Manx GP, Billy was also awarded trophies for the following: Fastest Lap; Best Newcomer; Best Local Rider; and Best Overall Performance.

Due to the requirement for him to return to Afghanistan at the end of his R&R period, Billy was not able to attend the awards ceremony to collect his trophies. Instead, he drove directly to RAF Brize Norton after the event and flew straight back out to Afghanistan.

Billy was a remarkable young soldier. He always made it clear that, although he was passionate about road racing, his Army career came first. He was a prime example of a modern-day paratrooper; professional, industrious, selfless, loyal and courageous. In 2014, he excelled in his military duties, and he secured the accolade of best private soldier in his Company. As a result of his outstanding soldiering ability and leadership potential, he was selected to attend the Potential Junior Non-Commissioned Officer cadre, where once again he excelled, receiving the highest grade – that of 'Distinction'. In Afghanistan on operations, he consistently proved that he was a most effective and capable private soldier, demonstrating on a daily basis the leadership qualities and skills of a Junior Non-Commissioned Officer.

Consequently, throughout the tour in 2014, he was employed as the mentor for an Afghan National Army platoon commander. This is true testament to Billy's maturity, positive attitude, military professionalism, and outstanding soldiering ability.

So why did I award Billy the Fishmongers' Trophy in 2014? In short, it was because he had successfully juggled an exceptionally busy operational and military work schedule with a demanding amateur road racing calendar over the previous twelve months. He had achieved the very highest of standards in both his professional and personal life and in both aspects, he had demonstrated the characteristics of a true paratrooper: determination, professionalism, and a constant desire to win. He tirelessly promoted The Parachute Regiment at every available opportunity, acting as the perfect ambassador for the Regiment, the British Army, and indeed the Armed Forces as a whole.

Billy embodied the ethos of The Parachute Regiment and as described by Viscount Montgomery of Alamein, the Regiment's second Colonel Commandant, he was the best of the best – 'Every man an Emperor'.

His Excellency Lieutenant General Sir John Lorimer KCB DSO MBE

Lieutenant Governor of the Isle of Man

Billy did manage to get home in March 2015 to race at Jurby on Martin Bullock's CBR600RR Honda and GSXR 750. He also had a practice spin out on the Collins & Russell Kawasaki KR1S that he would be using for the Classic TT. He managed to finish in the top 10 of four races.

Then in April he went to Oulton Park with Mally Oates and on the Honda, he had won the Newcomers on he managed a mixed bag of results: an 18th which he was very disappointed with and a 7th out of 34 starters at a track he never raced at before.

Billy also became a proud uncle in April as well. His niece, and our first grandchild, the gorgeous Evie Rose was born premature weighing only 4.9lbs on the 15th of April 2015. My, she was tiny, and she did go and support him later that year at Armoy in Ireland, which I know he was chuffed with.

Billy and Evie Rose

Evie Rose supporting Uncle Billy in Armoy

Billy was next racing at Tandragee in Ireland was the 2nd of May, he loved the Irish road racing whilst out on tour I sent

him regular copies of The Irish Road Racer. He qualified 6th for the Super sport 600 race and finished 6th, then in the Superbike he qualified 15th on his Honda 600, and in a very wet race finished 10th so he was happy enough with that. He loved Ireland; I wish we could have watched him more.

Race Face

Next was the Northwest 200, again on his CBR600RR. We managed to get over to watch him with some friends from the island and we had a great time, although Billy was to owe

Hannah and Becky a few drinks - he was on the starting grid when Hannah asked where his helmet and gloves were? 'In the van,' Billy said, with a look of sheer panic on his face.

Hannah ran back to the paddock followed by Becky who had the van keys. It was close, but he managed it. We all had a brilliant night out. Not totally sure where Billy went next, but I think he went back to camp/work.

Billy & Rhys having a chill

NW200 Pit Crew

He arrived back on the Island ready to do the post TT on the 13th of June at the Southern 100 circuit in Castletown. It was a try out for the Martin Bullock Honda 600 and Suzuki 750 that he would be riding at the Southern100 in July and the Manx Grand Prix in August. The weather was good, and he finished 4th in the 600 race behind James Cowton, Jamie Coward and Adrian Harrison. Then in the 1100 race he was 5th, but the first 750 home, so not a bad effort.

Southern 100 Billy #24 Michael Dunlop #3

Then 20th & 21st of June it was off to Oliver's Mount in Scarborough for the Barry Sheen Cup. Billy finished 4th on the Saturday behind Ivan Lintin, Daley Mathieson and James Neesom. Then on the Sunday, a 5th behind Lintin, Cowton, Gooding's and Hankin. He was happy with that because it was done on his trusty Newcomers winning bike, still with the still sealed engine from 2014.

Billy came home in July for the Southern 100 race in Castletown, which he loved watching and loved riding. It was the last shakedown for the Martin Bullock bikes before the Manx Grand Prix, so no pressure there. He had four races, two on the Suzuki 750 and two on the Honda 600 he finished best newcomer in all 4 races. He ended up on Crash DVD with his big off.

Billy (53) went over to Armoy 24th & 25th July, Super sport race 1 saw him finish 10th behind Andy Lawson 8th and James Cowton 9th the second race saw him 8th behind Andy Lawson (10) again. Andy sadly lost his life at the Ulster Grand Prix in August and James (52) was involved in a fatal accident at the Southern 100 in July 2018. Also, Davy Morgan (71) lost his life at the 2022 TT.

RIP

Chapter 8

Don't ask for an easier life ask to be a better person (Bette Davis)

Martin Bullock who ran The Full Factory Racing Team provided Billy with two bikes to ride the Junior and Senior Manx Grand Prix, a Honda 600 and a Suzuki 750. Practice proved to be a similar duel carried on from last year, with Billy and Malachi trading fastest laps. Billy also was riding in the Classic TT on the Collins and Russel Kawasaki KR1S 250.

The Gooseneck on the KR1S

On the Monday 31st August Billy set off in the Classic TT and did and standing start lap of 101.9mph, then when approaching Keppel Gate ran out of fuel on his second lap. Gutted wasn't the word. He got a lift back to the grandstand in the course inspection car driven by Gavin Corkill, who had sponsored him for the last 2 years.

There was an evening practice and Billy had decided to go out for a lap on the Suzuki 750 which was for Friday's Senior race. Disaster struck approaching Sarah's Cottage on the exit of Glen Helen. He went to overtake a slower rider, got out too wide and ended up high siding himself at 100+ mph. An Air med helicopter took him to Nobles Hospital, where after Xray's he was discharged with everything intact. The Suzuki however didn't fare as well (sorry Andy Grimshaw), it was trashed, so the plan was to run the Honda in both Wednesday's Junior race and Fridays Senior.

Tuesday came and Billy was sore, with a capital S, but after some physio (thank you Scott's physio Peel) said he was fit enough to race on Wednesday. So came the Junior race, once again Billy and Malachi swapped places all race but a mechanical issue saw Mal run on at the Creg Ny Baa and lose precious seconds. Billy came past the Gooseneck on the last lap P1 +10. 1st Position 10 second lead. Only about 13 miles to go, he backed it off slightly over the mountain for the last time but almost too much as he crossed the line only beating Mal by 1.8 seconds an almost identical margin for last year's Newcomer's race.

Jumping Ballaugh Bridge 1st Practice

Loving Life.

More drama was to come in Friday's Senior race, with Billy a lot less sore now he was looking forward to another duel with Mal.

Once again, they were swapping places from the start of the race, but on lap 3 Billy was given a 30 second penalty for overtaking on a yellow flag which after talking to him about it, he had no option as there was nowhere for him to go. It was not to matter in the end as a mechanical issue on lap 4 in Ramsey brought Billy's race to an early end, Mal went on to be a deserving victor. Sadly, Malachi also was fatally injured at the Northwest 200 races in Ireland in the May of 2016.

DNF Manx Grand Prix Senior 2015

Billy and Malachi

Bottom of Bray Hill (That's fibreglass dust off the fairing)

Malachi Mitchel Thomas **OUT OUT**

That Friday evening was the awards presentation at the Villa Marina in Douglas and what a night it was, we left Billy, Malachi, Hannah and Rhys Hardisty to it, they went "OUT OUT pushing each other down the road in supermarket trollies! How old were they?

In September it was off to Oliver's Mount for the Gold cup on the 12th and 13th, we went across for that and met up with my mum and my brother and his family, which was nice. The weather was poor on the Saturday and Billy ended up sliding off the bike at the Esses, he was alright, but the bike needed some work. Between Billy, Rhys and Dave they managed to get it back together and a big thank you to Dean Harrison who popped his head in and managed to talk Billy into "getting back out there".

So, Sunday Billy ended up finishing 2nd behind Dan Kneen who also is sadly no longer with us. Then a respectable 15th in the Steve Henshaw Gold Cup.

Billy's cousins Catrin & Ben Scarborough 2015

The next event for Billy was in New Zealand the Suzuki Tri Series, 3 races in December at Hampton Downs, Manfeild and the Cemetery Circuit on Boxing Day. He had the loan of a Kawasaki ZXR600 from Marcus Begley who ran Biggles Racing. We decided we would go out there and watch him Leanne would travel out there on her own and meet up with Billy and Hannah. Dave and I and our friend Mark would meet them at the apartment in Queenstown we had a fantastic time, I beat Billy at luging something I would not let him forget! Leanne and I overcame our fear of heights to do it. The following day Dave and Ringo did the Bungie jump in Queenstown, Billy had done it the year before, so Dave had to do it. We decided we would go to puzzle world in Wanaka, which was not too far away but, on a winding, high road and Billy was driving omg, he had been out drinking Guinness the night before and decided it would be good fun to fart and lock all the windows I have never felt so sick. On Christmas Day we all got invited to Flea and Julies house which was a bit weird sitting outside having a big Christmas Brunch, but it was brilliant another fantastic memory.

Christmas Day Brunch in the sun at Julie & Flea's

Boxing Day was awesome as well watching racing in the sunshine and seeing the smile on my son's face, I almost forgave him for locking the windows. Billy and Hannah left New Zealand before us to celebrate New Year, we went on to stay with friends and went into Sydney to bring in the New year in. I am so glad we went out there and watched him as 14 weeks later he was no longer with us.

Living the Dream with Marcus Beagley at Whanganui

Chapter 9

'There is no wealth but life'

(John Ruskin)

In 2016 Billy came home for the southern 100 launch in February, he got talking to Peter Hillaby who at the time ran Auto 66 at Scarborough he offered to pay Billy to ride there in the Spring Cup in April, he was made up at getting paid to ride it, although we had reservations as at the time it wasn't being run very well, he was an adult and made his own choices. We saw Billy again when he came over in March for the newcomer's weekend he met up with Rhys. We also went for a walk with our 3 border collies and Evie Rose in her pram, he loved acting like a big kid with his dog Nip, I remember taking the micky out of him for his birthday cake from Hannah that she put on face book of him blowing his candles out. We crammed a lot into those few days, and I am grateful that we did, it would be the last time we saw him.

Happy 25th Birthday Billy

Billy had got himself a new bike for the 2016 season a ZX10R, I saw a picture of it, it looked awesome, he had his helmet done by stickboy, Phil Bradbury in poppies for the parachute regiment.

The army had given him a year off to pursue his racing carrier. He wanted to do the TT and had been backed by Des and Dot Collins he had been given a ride on Jack Valentines Valmoto 675 MV Augusta he was living the dream. Carl Cox had mentioned he may sponsor him for the TT, Billy got chatting to him in New Zealand.

We were all proud and excited for him, we all knew the danger we had just virtually rode the grand prix with him. It was an exciting time for him and Hannah, they were buying a house together and Hannah was starting social work training.

On Thursday evening Billy put some photos on face book with the quote when your girlfriend goes food shopping! all the things Hannah had bought to take to Oliver's Mount on the Friday and there were lots, but they were both pleased to be in the race bus, ambo with electricity and no holes in the roof.

On the Friday Billy sent me a picture of Hannah at the shop, with a quote when your girlfriend leaves all the food for the weekend in the fridge! You buy more, he sent a picture of Hannah at the petrol station buying more. I told him it was a joint effort I also asked if he had rung his sister as it was Evie Rose's 1st birthday, he had. That was the last message I sent him.

The Last Photograph

Chapter 10

Why? Why Not? Why Not You? Why Not You Now? (Asian)

Six years on from that day trying to remember is difficult. I am told by people in the know, that it's my brain blocking out the trauma, but here goes. I will write my version of THAT time, but Dave's will probably be different.

FRIDAY 15th April 2016

MY FRIDAY 15th

I can remember having a bad day at work, and vowing to find another job, I was too old to take this s---, it was my granddaughters 1st birthday on the 15th, so Dave and I were going to see her after work.

That night Billy texted Dave to say everything was okay they were in the rock star paddock with the transponder charging and just one point of the ambo roof was leaking, so all good.

I can't recall what I did on the Saturday, I do know Dave was at Jurby scrutineering and we went to the local pub for a teatime pint. Billy rang Dave I don't know what was said as the reception was bad and Dave had to go outside, he just said that the track was very greasy and difficult to enjoy.

The following day Dave was scrutineering again at Jurby, my daughter Leanne and I were training to do the parish walk to raise money for the Parachute Regiment, when I got a call from Dave saying Hannah had rung him, Billy's race had been red flagged for the second time and Billy was still not back at the ambo.

Leanne and I carried on walking trying to convince ourselves all would be fine, telling myself Dave would ring me saying Billy was fine but the bike not, hmm? What about TT or worse Billy injured and couldn't ride the TT? We plodded on for another mile or so, different scenarios playing in my head.

Dave rang back and it was worse than anything I had imagined. Billy was hurt big time - a head injury - he was being taken to Scarborough hospital and Hannah was being driven there by a lady called Janice from the paddock whom she had only just met.

It was there and then that I felt Billy had died. We had had conversations around injuries he might receive in his line of work or sport, he always said "switch me off". Of course, you never think you will be in that situation.

I rang our other daughter Kerry who luckily was at home, she came and collected us and the dogs and drove us back home and Dave rang to say he too was on his way home. Everything felt surreal.

Billy had now been helicoptered to Middlesbrough Hospital as they were better equipped for head injuries, Hannah was being driven by the police to Middlesbrough.

I looked around my kitchen at the Sunday lunch I had prepped for us - that went to the dogs. Next, we had to get to the UK. Easier said than done on a Sunday, no boat and the airport shut at 9pm.

That's when my heart broke, I just curled up on Billy's bed with Brown Ted and sobbed. Dave came in and said he had been in touch with Ringo, Billy's mate in camp, and someone will ring us.

I don't remember much about the next few hours. I know I rang work, then my friend Christine asking if she could look after my cats, chickens, ducks and rabbit. The girls took the dogs to kennels. I don't recall ringing family, only talking to my sister-in-law Helen in Wales who said she would drive up to Billy in Middlesbrough. I asked her to tickle his feet and pull his toes as I used to do that when he was hung over and wouldn't move out of bed.

An army padre called Jonathon rang to tell us there would be a helicopter or plane waiting for us at Ronaldsway airport, the ladies shouldn't wear anything floaty, and a car would pick us up. It was at this point I said Well Billy won't need a bloody toilet bag or change of clothes will he, he's dead.

I don't know why but I got a packet of crisps, Brown Ted, so called because he's brown (the imagination of a two-year-old), and my gardening pants and was ready to leave. I don't even know if I took a change of clothes, I have no recollection of packing a bag anyway. The Taxi arrived to collect us, I can remember thinking to myself Billy will never be coming here again.

We collected the girls on the way to the airport, when we arrived, I remember seeing two fire engines on the runway. Dave said they had to be there once the airport is open. We were escorted to a little room I think I had a cup of tea, then the Army Air Corp arrived with a 6-seater 'tin can' aircraft. We were given a safety briefing on the apron and then flown to Newcastle.

There was no security checks or ID when we arrived, and we were kept in a private lounge while we waited for the taxi. It seemed very surreal. We were then driven to the hospital in Middlesbrough to be met at the doors by padre Jonathon and Paul the Hat, whom we became very close to over the coming weeks (soldiers other than paras are known as crap hats as they don't wear the maroon beret).

After introductions we walked up to the intensive care unit. I can remember it was a six or eight bed ward and we had to put horrible plastic gowns on to go in.

My heart broke when I saw my big strong son lying so helpless, I felt useless. As a mum you save them from pain, you protect them no matter what age they are. I turned to Dave and said he's gone there's nothing behind his eyes, Dave replied yep. he's done it this time.

We sat with him for a while then went to the family waiting room, which had a toilet and sink and a bed settee. I can remember expecting someone to come and talk to me, give me a leaflet, book anything just someone in the know to put an arm around me and explain, to tell us what to do in this situation. Once again it was the army and padre that did.

I was hurting because Billy's friends had arrived before us, as had family, Dave's sister Ann and husband Mark - I think they were in their campervan in the car park. Hannah's dad was also there, and I was angry they were all there before us and I was angry at everything including Billy.

I wanted to go and sit with him, hold his hand and chat to him but I knew it was pointless. It just hurt so much. I think part of me was waiting for him to sit up and say 'what's all the fuss?

I could murder a bine', but I knew that wasn't going to happen so Dave and I went for a walk.

I saw a bottle of Glenfiddich whisky in a random corner shop, it always reminds me of Billy, so Dave bought me one. Time meant nothing to me, day night evening all fell into oblivion I cannot recall when the doctor said they wanted to know if we would donate his organs.

I wasn't prepared to be asked and I said no, he was my child and I wanted to keep him whole. Everyone else in the family and Hannah said Billy had wanted to donate his organs. I knew that because ever since he was little, he'd say 'they're no good to me when I am dead mum' but it was the only thing I had any control over.

Of course, I relented a little later as time was of the essence. I then decided I wasn't going to eat - again it was a control thing, and I didn't eat for two days. I sat in the stairwell with Dave and Helen and cried and screamed. Then I could hear Billy in my head saying, 'get a grip mum', so I decided I was going to be strong like Christina Schmid. She came across as a very proud lady when her husband Ollie (Olaf) was killed in Afghanistan in 2009, whilst trying to disarm an IED, I haven't a clue where it came from or why, I just decided I would try to do him proud, that's what I hope I did and continue to do.

I cannot remember what day we switched Billy off. I know the nurses were brilliant they cut some of his hair and put it in a little keepsake box for us and they did handprints of Mum, Dad & Billy. I asked if it would be possible for us to do a toast around his bed and play 'Ride of the Valkyries'.

They agreed then we had the hunt for small cups so my brother Neil and I went down to Costa and got a few and the nurses gave us some pill pots!

I don't know how many bottles of Glenfiddich the lads brought! The nurses pulled the curtains round and we found the music on someone's phone, and we toasted him with 'always up, never down' 'forever side by side' and 'Utrinique Paratus' the Parachute Regiment motto which means "Ready for anything".
The lads and family said their farewells, then it was just us 4 and time to remove his tubes. I said silent prayers that he would let a big sigh out and breathe but he didn't play along. So, we said our goodbyes. I am in awe of the families who lost loved ones in conflict and never got to kiss and hug them at the end.
The days after we all sat in the bar in the evenings the lad's telling tales of what they all got up to with Billy. I can remember that the singer Prince had died, and it was also the Queen's birthday on the 21st. I got sick and tired of listening to it on repeat on the hotel TV. It seemed to be on very loud but to be fair, all your senses are heightened, and everything annoys you.

A lot of what I can remember comes back in flashes, like someone holding flash cards. The one day we did go out we went to O'Connell's bar at lunch time to meet up with Billy's mates and my brother and wife. We arrived a little later and were shocked to find they were all laughing but we soon found out why, it was because Alec Isaacs had sat down to eat his meal and the full plate of food just slid off the table onto his lap and the floor! They were all saying it was just like Billy had walked past and pushed it off the table. It's little moments like these that make me smile now. If what his friends say about his antics are true, it probably is what he would have done to Isaacs!

Well, what do we do now, we had a bit of a routine going for what seemed like weeks not days, Kerry wanted to go home to Martin and her baby and flew home, we decided to go to my brothers in Colwyn Bay, so we hired a car and just the three of us Dave and I and Leanne left later that day. We all went walking, drank too much and didn't eat or sleep enough, just in disbelief really.

Chapter 11
A lifetime of training for just ten seconds (Jesse Owens)
That Week by Dave

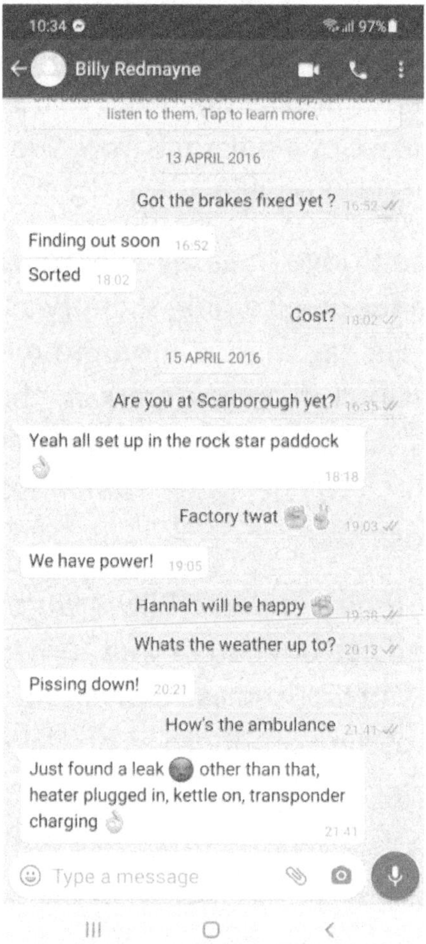

Friday 15th April 2016

Saturday 16th April 2016

I was scrutineering at Jurby for a two-day event, it was a pretty uneventful day. Cold but fine, I'd taken my iPad and hot-spotted it to my phone to watch the live timing at Oliver's Mount. Conditions weren't great there that day there were quite a few crashes. But Billy managed to qualify third row for the Spring Cup race. Got a message from Sue "Fancy a teatime pint"? "Sounds good" I replied.

Later whilst in the Bridge in Laxey Billy called me, doom and gloom. "It's like a fucking ice rink, slippery as fuck, had to pull out of one race" He had a good moan to me and I said, "If it doesn't feel right pull it up and park it, there's no point in taking risks this early in the season." "But I need the signatures for the TT!" he said, "Don't worry I'll be fine" Famous last words. ☹

That was the last time I spoke to Billy; I wish so dearly that he had of taken my advice but you cannot turn the clock back. He was determined and focused as he always was with whatever tasks lay in front of him. Stubborn as an Ox. Brave as Lion.

Sunday 17th April 2016

Off to Jurby again for me at 07:30, a good morning's scrutineering under my belt, I set up the iPad again and with one eye on the racing at Jurby I watched the events at Scarborough unfold. First race for Billy he came in 5th, happy days. That'll do.

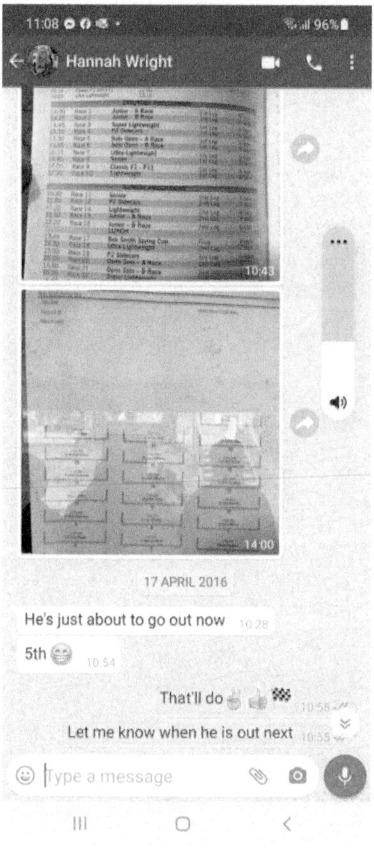

After lunch racing resumed at Jurby and Olivers Mount, it was bright and sunny by then at both racetracks. So, I sat watching the live timing of the Bob Smith Spring Cup race.

It started and was red flagged almost immediately, a rider had crashed and needed to be moved to the Medical Centre and the track needed clearing up.

The rest of the riders grouped up back at the start line and waited for a restart. The race restarted and I was watching it on the live timing, Red Flag again! I messaged Hannah and this is how it played out.

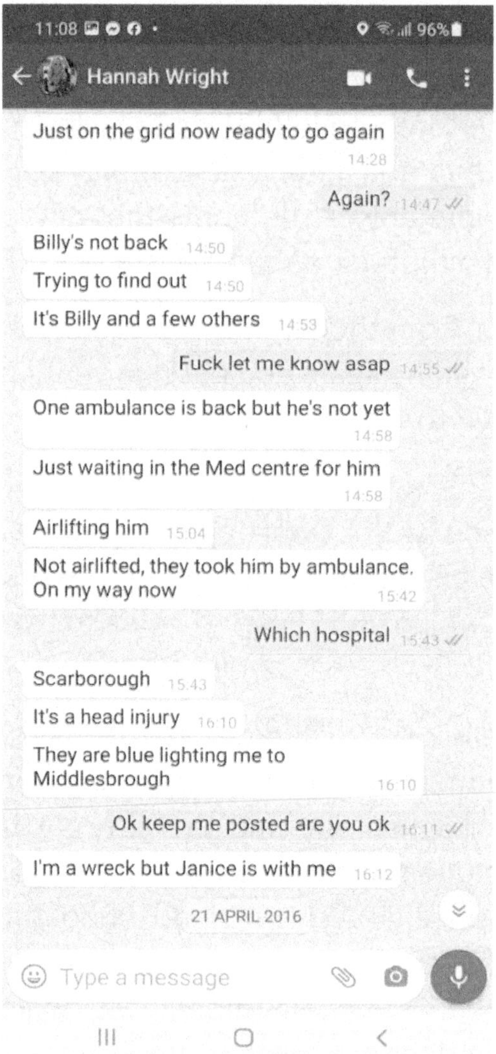

The longest hour and twenty minutes of my life.

Turns out the Red Flag was put out so the ambulance at the Esses could proceed to the Medical Centre to drop some morphine off for an injured rider, ironic thing is it only got as far as the Back Straight as that's where the pile up that ultimately killed Billy happened.

One rider had seen the Red Flag and shut off, but a following rider didn't react as quickly and clipped the rear wheel of the bike in front the careered left taking Billy down with him. The following pack had nowhere to go and Billy got hit. I don't for one minute blame any of the riders that day, they were just tangled up in a multitude of bad decisions.

The paramedics from the ambulance did a fantastic job, they got Billy's heart going again and got him ventilated and stable enough to move to Scarborough hospital. The next five days were a rollercoaster of emotions.

I phoned Sue, she was out walking with Leanne and told them there had been an accident and that Billy was involved. Kerry went to pick them up and I headed home to Laxey and started making phone calls.

One of the calls was to Ringo one of Billy's mates in his platoon, I asked him to let whoever at camp know what had happened. Then when Sue and the girls got back, we went into planning mode of how we were going to get off the island and to Middlesbrough ASAP. I tried to book flights, no joy. I tried to book the ferry, no joy. In desperation I booked a sailing for Monday 08:45 to Heysham, we were taking the campervan. The dogs got taken to the kennels and Kerry and Leanne went home to pack.

Sue had called her brother Neil in North Wales and his wife Helen said she would head up to the hospital straight away and I had spoken to my sister Ann in Lancashire, and she said that they would go up as well. Hannah was already at the hospital with her dad Steve. So at least she had some support straight away.

About eight o'clock my mobile rang, it was a Staff Sergeant from camp, "how far are you from the airport Mr Redmayne and how many will be travelling" I replied about 20 miles but the last flights from the island have gone, and the airport closes about 9pm. "No sir the airport will be open for you, we are trying to arrange transport now. Please pack a case each and make sure you do not wear loose clothing." I thought to myself what the actual F##K is going on. About two hours later another call from the sergeant to confirm a taxi had been booked to pick us all up and take us to the airport, there would be an Army transport aircraft picking us up, flying to Newcastle and then we would be transferred to the hospital by taxi. Shit the bed, these people were moving mountains for us.

Monday 18th April 2016

Around 1am the taxi arrived in we jumped with our hastily packed and Sue clutching Brown Ted, off to pick up Kerry and Leanne and down to the airport. I have worked at the airport, so I know about the security setup but when we arrived we were dropped at the gate that takes you directly onto the apron, we were taken into the gate lodge, a quick check of our passports and told to wait. I could hear the security guy on the phone to various people who had been called out to open the airport. Around half an hour later a small twin engine Army Air Corps aircraft landed and taxied to a halt a hundred yards from the gate lodge. We were escorted out to the aircraft and two very nice young men gave us a safety briefing of the do's and don'ts during the flight. It was surreal to say the least, but we piled in strapped up and trundled off down the runway.

The flight itself was very noisy and cold, we had headphones on so I could hear the pilot chatter. Pilot to co-pilot "Have you ever landed at Newcastle" co-pilot back "Nah, but I'm sure we'll be fine" An hour later touchdown and taxied up to a private lounge, ushered out of the aircraft we said our thank you's and they wished Billy luck and a speedy recovery. Time for a comfort break and a cup of tea and the taxi arrived. I then took a phone call from a man who will be my friend forever, Padre Jonathon. He explained that we were about an hour away from the hospital and for me to call him on our arrival and he would talk us in. One hour later I called him, and he directed the taxi driver to the correct entrance, as I said we're here the door opened and there was Padre, the next few days were the most heart wrenching of my life.

It was about 5am, when we first went into ICU. Soon as I saw him all wired up and, on a ventilator, I said to myself "well you've gone and done it proper this time". Hannah was by his side and Sue sat on the other side of the bed, there we stayed for a time I still can't measure. The ICU staff were brilliant and over the next few hours a steady stream of people arrived to see Billy so there was always at least three people with him. The day was like wading through treacle, each movement was like slow motion.

Friends and family arrived steadily until we had virtually taken over the family room, the Para guys kept appearing with the odd bottle of Glenfiddich which was a distraction. Hic. Padre was an absolute rock throughout the day.

I kept getting messages from well-wishers throughout the morning, then one of the girls said it had been on Manx Radio that Billy was in ICU very poorly but breathing for himself! I was fucking livid; it was as plain as day that no one from either Auto 66 or the ACU had been arsed to put a correct press release out. After a phone call to a friend on the island who was heavily involved with the MGP a press release went out.

I spoke at length with the consultant in ICU and he explained that Billy's brain had taken such an impact that the damage was beyond any chance of repair. I thought back to all the bangs on the head he'd had over his twenty-five years, from falling off a bench as a toddler to knocking himself senseless at Knock Froy motocross track. This time the cat's ninth life was up.

We had to make a decision, the hardest one as a parent you would ever have to make. Billy had opted to be an organ donor and had said to both me and Sue "don't keep me alive for the sake of it if I get a slice" So after a long talk with Hannah, Kerry and Leanne the decision was made for his life support to be withdrawn. There were loads of forms to be filled in and discussions with the organ donor nurses, but we got through it. Everybody was gathered up in the family room and we told them all our decision. There were gasps and tears but there was no other option.

Tuesday 19th April 2016

Just after midnight 34 of us gathered round his bed in ICU, all armed with a tot of whiskey in an array of receptacles from paper cups to pill pots. Lex set his phone on Billy's chest and started the music. Wagner's Ride of the Valkyries the Para's theme tune. As the music ended, we all raised our glasses etc. to him and took our shots.

Everybody then dispersed and left the family alone, at about 2am the nurse in charge of Billy started the process of withdrawing his life support. If anybody has been through this experience my heart goes out to them, to watch all the monitors connected to your loved one slowly drop down to no activity is absolutely devastating.

Finally, the nurse said right we are going to have to move him so he can get to the theatre to have his organs removed, letting him go was unbelievable hard but we knew he was going to help someone else. We left ICU like zombies, the Padre and Paul were there outside and they ushered us to the minibus and took us to our hotel in Middlesbrough. That was that, he was gone. ☹

We got up and went down to breakfast, the mood was surreal. As I chewed on what to all intents and purposes was a lump of cardboard or so it seemed a lady who was waiting on said to us "I know where you are just now, I lost my son last year. He was only 15, he got stabbed and died". I thought to myself how Billy had lived his life and died doing something he loved, and this young lad had had his life torn away from him. There was no comparison, our grief was immense but hers you could not start to imagine.

Sue said to me that she wanted to go and see Billy, so I spoke to Padre Jonathon, and he said he would get in touch with the hospital. He arranged a visit for around 12 noon, the viewing room where Billy was wasn't in the nicer places of the hospital. We had to walk through the service corridors near the kitchens and all we could smell was cooking vegetables it was not pleasant. We were led into this room with a small sofa in it and a door into another room. Shortly this door opened, and we were asked to come through to where Billy was, I wish I had not seen him that day. To be fair to the hospital they had not had much time to prepare him but that sight of him has stayed with me since.

We went back to the hotel and just sat their shell shocked. Sue wouldn't eat anything as she was in a right state. I was just going over the events of the last couple of days in my head and couldn't understand how this crash had happened. I told Sue that I needed to go to Scarborough. We spoke together as a family and decided that tomorrow we would go to Oliver's Mount and try and get some answers. Hannah had decided to go and see Billy on the next day so we would go with Padre and Paul.

In the hotel bar that night we had a good old booze up for Billy but no matter how much I drank I was unable to get drunk, I think it's just the way your body is functioning in times of great stress.

Wednesday 20th April.

After another breakfast that went down like eating cardboard, we piled into the minibus. Me and Sue, Kerry, Leanne, the Padre and Paul ready for the trip to Scarborough, I didn't know how this day would go. We stopped off to get supplies for a picnic lunch I was hoping Sue would eat something, but she said no to wanting anything.

It was about a 2-hour drive with a couple of comfort breaks, then the "Dreaded Mount" arose in front of us. We came up through the paddock, and on to the circuit, it's a public road normally. Round the Mere hairpin, up Sheen's Rise, right round Esses In along to the left of Esses out and on to the Back Straight.

As we approached the crash site my mouth dried up like a desert, it's an awful feeling being where your son lost his life. But at least he didn't die in Afghanistan because I wouldn't have been able to go there. We got out of the minibus, and I started to try and get a mental picture of what had happened four days previously. Sue and the girls were looking at the tree that the Kawasaki had hit on its journey after it left Billy's control. People had been placing flowers and photos there. I was walking the police markings trying to figure out how an accident had happened there on a straight part of the track, it would all become apparent when the truth about the accident came out at the inquest.

We walked down the track to Memorial In the left hander at the end of the Back Straight. There is a viewpoint there overlooking Scarborough and it looked like a favourite place for scattering ashes. It was quite peaceful and we all felt a bit of Billy was there with us. Suddenly Sue said, "I feel like Fish and Chips on the seafront and a game of "Wooshie Wooshie" (it's what a very young Billy called air hockey).

So down into Scarborough on to the promenade and a restaurant was found and fish and chips was had, it was great to see Sue able to eat something, I think going to the circuit did us all a world of good. After a few games of air hockey and a pint of Guinness we jumped back into the minibus and Paul drove us back to Middlesborough.

We had a few beers that night and "rinsed" the Padre for takeaway pizza. We all felt a little better, Hannah had been to see Billy and saw that our trip to Oliver's Mount had done us good, so she asked the lads (Lex, Ash, Al, Ringo and Chris) to go with her tomorrow.

Thursday 21st April.

Hannah and the lads set off early to Scarborough, we were in limbo. Waiting for a call from the hospital regarding when we get Billy home. We walked around Middlesborough city centre like zombies, the shock of everything was sinking in. After lunch Padre phoned the hospital to find out what was going on, they couldn't give him a definite day Billy would be released as there was the autopsy to be done.

We had a family discussion and decided that Kerry would fly back to the island and me, Sue and Leanne would hire a car and go to North Wales for the weekend and stay at Neil and Helen's. When Hannah and the lads returned from Scarborough, we agreed it was for the best that we leave the hotel as it wasn't doing us any good being there.

So, our last night involved a few beers and a good old reminisce about Billy, and fleecing the Padre again.

Friday 22nd April.

We checked out of the hotel and said our farewells to the lads and Hannah, Kerry went off with Paul and Padre to Liverpool and we went to hire a car. The drive down to Neil and Helen's was a drudge, only an annoying stop off at the noisiest motorway services known to man. I swear people were doing it on purpose to piss me off. My filters had gone!

Friday night was spent talking around the kitchen table of what had happened "That Week" and more whiskey was consumed. We were all just shell shocked by it. The next step for us was to get Billy back home but what a struggle that would turn out to be!

Chapter 12

Life is like a coin. You can spend it any way you wish, but you only spend it once. (Lillian Dickson)

Then it was time to return to the island, I didn't want to leave him behind, even though I knew he was dead it just felt wrong. Arriving at our house was awful, I could hear him see him and smell him even though he didn't live with us on a permanent basis, I could feel his presence. I went outside to check on the ducks, hens and rabbits and friends of ours had left bags of shopping in the utility all the necessities you could need, brilliant I didn't have to face anyone yet. What a lovely surprise from lovely thoughtful people, Phil and Marie Wales you rock. We also had lots of lovely flowers from friends in Australia, New Zealand and the UK, nothing really sank in who the cards or letters were from we had some nice letters handwritten from the Army.

A little later I have no idea how long after we were home, but we got a phone call from padre asking if they could remove Billy's brain, well I don't think anything can prepare you for that! I screamed cried, why can't they just let him be, he's donated his organs, just let him lie and be my handsome little soldier, Dave rang Hannah to see what her thoughts were, we decided if we did let them go ahead, we could probably have his funeral sooner and we agreed that lighter is faster. We had people who wanted to come to the funeral that were racing at the Northwest 200 in Ireland in May, and it was nearly the end of April we had to get him home and plan a funeral, how the hell do we do that it's not there's a handbook! Once again, the Army stepped in and sorted plane tickets and a car for the four of us to see him in the chapel of rest in Liverpool.

We were traveling on rows 13 seats a, b, c, and d eeek! We think Billy was setting us up for a rocky day. "Paul the hat "met us when we landed and took us to the chapel of rest, the girls came in but didn't want to see Billy, so Dave and I went through to the viewing room, I had to look twice at Billy he had a white shirt and red tie on with his hands placed on his chest holding a plastic red rose, well there was no stopping me and my mouth I turned to Dave what the F---, he looks like he's 15 and going to bloody school, (at his secondary school they had white shirt red tie) and why the hell has he got a bloody rose in his hand I went on and on then I heard a voice that seemed to come from a long way off, saying , we do try to do our best for them, there was a lady sat discreetly in a corner ! oh dear cheers for that Bill I felt awful but I could just picture him laughing, we made our exit. We went to the docks in Liverpool and met up with everyone, Issacs drove Billy's ambo from Yorkshire as Hannah's dad Steve had it, poor Issacs swore he would never drive it again, it was a beast to drive. Lex and Hannah arrived in Billy's car which was amazing as spin either of them round and they're lost, and Chris and Ash brought a minibus over as they were staying on the island until after the funeral to support us, once again I can't thank the SFSG and Churchill lines charity for all they did for our family.
We all went to' Liverpool One' for food, and then back to the docks to wait for Billy to arrive in a van to be taken to the chapel of rest in Onchan. We waited and waited he still hadn't arrived, no answer at either funeral home when we rang, Hannah and I decided we would not get on the boat without him, by this time we had to check all the vehicles on the ferry, but in typical army fashion the clerk had booked the mini bus

on the 02.15 ferry from Heysham, a few phone calls and Ash and Chris were on with us, but where was Billy? last call for vehicles came and Chris went to find out where he was, Billy apparently had been the first on the ferry 2hrs ago!

Once again, we arrived home everything felt weird, but I consoled myself that I could go and sit and chat to Billy and put him in his ventilated hole ridden para top, jeans and his boots and not a plastic flower in sight. We now had the funeral party rooms and crematorium to book, Dave Hannah and I agreed that the Villa Marina in Douglas was ideal, and the girls agreed, it is walking distance from the crematorium and easy parking. We decided we needed 2 rooms upstairs for the army and friends and downstairs a quieter room for family and children. We now needed a date where all the times matched the only day was Friday the 13th may, I cried and said no way! Dave and I then looked at each other and said, yep go on then he would love it, everything fell into place then, with the crematorium, funeral director, venue and catering, so just the last lap round the TT course to organise and a change of clothes for Billy, job done. Hannah and I took Billy his holey para tee ventilation Billy said jeans and his cowboy boots, we went back to the funeral home a couple of days later to see him and say our goodbyes, my he smelt vile but Hannah had brought some of his after shave as he was slowly getting worse during the week she applied it all over, it was a bit better we went in separately to say our last good byes it was bloody heart breaking knowing I would never hear his silly laugh have a hug or him ring me with a "Mother how goes it" it hurt so much.

I had decided I wanted to take Billy in the back of the ambulance for his last lap. Ken Faragher funeral director said it was fine ,but I knew it had a dodgy hand brake and that we had chosen the Gooseneck as a special spot for the army to lay there wreaths, how silly of us, it's very much shaped like a goose neck long with a twist hence its name I had visions of Billy sliding out of the back and ploughing into the bikes etc like a comedy sketch but truthfully I was bloody panicking, I had no idea of how many bikes would turn up how long the tailback would be , but I could do this for him, couldn't I. I could hear him saying sort your shit out mum! so I went to see ken who told me to get the lads to bring the ambulance down and he would put some brackets in to hold the coffin, Mally our friend said he would sit in the back with billy in a garden chair and hold on to the coffin for me.

Sorted.

The days leading up to the funeral are all mixed up to me so what I write will more than likely be back to front and not in the right order! I can remember the paras Lex, Alec, Ash and Chris stayed at one of Billy's friends holiday lets in Glen Mona, not too far from us, they had a lot to organise, there were lots of friends from the military flying in from God knows where, some on the ferry. Padre Jonathon had managed to get the lads somewhere to sleep at the local cadet hall for those staying overnight. My brother his wife and children stayed in our camper van, my other brother and his family, Dave's sister and husband brought their own camper vans, Dave's nephews Joe and Henry stayed free of charge at our friend's pub the Queens in Laxey, the wonderful Marie had organised a room in the hotel that she managed for my mum, free of charge. All other family members stayed in Douglas in various hotels as did Hannah's friends and family. All seemed to be going well the wonderful Marie was sorting all the catering for us. I asked the local dog groomer Graham at 'Paws for Thought' in Ramsey if he could fit Nip, Billy's old dog in for a tart up on Friday 13th for me, my nephew Ben was taking him in the car for Billy's last lap, yes, he would collect him from our house and bring him back for us in plenty of time for the funeral, and he didn't even charge us. There are some nice people about.

Neil, Ben and Nip

Well, here we are the morning of our son's funeral, Dave was taking Kerry on the back of his Firestorm, Leanne was going on the back of Billy's friend Ringo. Hannah and I in the ambulance (race bus), Mally a friend was going to sit in the back as planned in the garden chair to hold on to the coffin just in case and for my peace of mind. I can remember a few people standing on the side of the road as we drove through Laxey to the funeral home in Onchan, once there I had to reverse the ambo down to the doors to put the coffin in and to bolt it down, talk about panicking, then I heard an almighty loud unidentifiable noise I thought the ambo had blown a gasket, but one of Billy's acquaintance's in the RAF had got a Tornado and flew it past the grandstand wings swept back and full afterburners on as it dipped its wings at the grandstand, how absolutely amazing.

Me and Hannah on his last lap

Then it was time to set off, I think I swore all the way from the home to the grandstand, the ambo was a beast to drive more so when your upset. I didn't realise we were supposed to go slowly all the way round the track, it's not like it was a hearse. People we never even knew lined the course to pay their respects it was heart breaking for me but nice of people to remember him, I can remember seeing an elderly gentleman para standing at the church at Crosby and saluting, brought a tear to my eye it was a lovely gesture. Hannah kept telling me how many bikes were behind us, also we didn't have to wait for the traffic lights. As we came through Kirk Michael into Ballaugh I said to Hannah shall we go airborne over the bridge yes, so we did completely forgetting about Mally in the back in his deck chair all we heard was some choice words as we landed with a thud his bottled water went airborne along with Billy's beret and union jack off the coffin other than that all ok, or so we thought I would find out 6years later from Ian Billy's mechanic and friend, that when the para lads who were pole bearers found it difficult to carry the coffin and had to adjust and move people, even though they had practiced, it wasn't until I relayed the "airborne tale" that Ian laughed and said I must have shook Billy as we landed and all his weight had shifted that's why it was so difficult, oops but we had a laugh and said a typical Bill joke.

We managed to make it to the Gooseneck with no dramas, I remember seeing my friend Rachel and her son Aaron just off Parliament Square, Aaron idolised Billy and one day Billy popped into Rachels for a bru much to little Aarons delight, he sat and chatted to him for a while, anyway at the Gooseneck I was as calm as I could be.

Hannah jumped out for the laying of the wreathes Mally stayed in with me , I don't know what he could have done had the ambo started to roll, but she didn't, the wreathes that they laid where from, SFSG, PARACHHUTE REGIMENT, SAS, and OFFICERS OF ALL RANKS, one sad proud mum. We finally arrived at the grandstand, I asked Dave if he spotted a banner on hay bales on the run down from the Creg Na Ba saying fly high Billy Redmayne, we found out much later it was Lottie the mum of Billy's friends Jack and Ozzy Moore, it was so nice to see it, a few months later we went and retrieved it. I still have it somewhere.

The Gooseneck

Creg Ny Baa

Well, this is it I thought as we went to get freshened up in the Manx Grand Prix offices someone gave me a tot of whisky nice, and we followed my sons coffin to the crematorium, he got the full military honours, gun salute and last post not that I can remember much.

As horrible as it sounds, I wish someone had recorded it as I can only remember bits and whilst writing this, I am annoyed everyone records a wedding why not a funeral again it is that taboo, I would love to see all the people that turned out for him, maybe not in the first years but definitely now. Billy had picked his own music for his funeral, we did always joke about what music would be good when we die, he knew mine is “Down in a hole” by Alice in chains, his dads “Hell ain’t a bad place to be” by AC DC so when Lex said to us what Billy had picked, we were not surprised at all.

Jim, Bill's mate sorted all the PA etc for us, I do recall having a moment going through the crematorium doors seeing Padre, and hearing Jimmy Hendrix Voodoo Child blasting out,

followed by The Ride Of The Valkyries by Wagner, after the tributes Pearl Jam Alive, and as he went through the curtain AC DC Highway To Hell, in a funny way it made it easier that he had had an input in his funeral.

OFFICIAL PROGRAMME

FRIDAY 13th MAY 2016

Please stand as the Bearer Party enter the Chapel

MUSIC

VOODOO CHILD - Jimi Hendrix

INTRODUCTION AND WELCOME

The Reverend Jonathon Daniel CF (UB)

TRIBUTE TO BILLY

from the Race Community

TRIBUTE TO LCPL BILLY REDMAYNE

by Lt Col A J E Truett MBE,

THE COLLECT OF THE AIRBORNE FORCES

May the defence of the Most High be above and beneath, around and within us, in our going out and in our coming in, in our rising up and in our going down, through all our days and all our nights, until the dawn when the Sun of Righteousness shall arise, with healing in His wings for the peoples of the world; through Jesus Christ our Lord. Amen

MUSIC

THE RIDE OF THE VALKYRIES - Wagner

TRIBUTE TO BILLY
READ BY KERRY REDMAYNE

Death is nothing at all
I have only slipped away into the next room
I am I and you are you
Whatever we were to each other
That we are still
Call me by my old familiar name
Speak to me in the easy way you always used
Put no difference into your tone
Wear no forced air of solemnity or sorrow
Laugh as we always laughed
At the little jokes we always enjoyed together
Play, smile, think of me,
Let my name be ever the household word that it always was
Let it be spoken without effort
Without the ghost of a shadow in it
Life means all that it ever meant
It is the same as it ever was
There is absolute unbroken continuity
What is death but a negligible accident?
Why should I be out of mind
Because I am out of sight?
I am waiting for you for an interval
Somewhere very near
Just around the corner.

A TRIBUTE TO BILLY
WRITTEN BY SUE REDMAYNE

Dave and I received a letter from friends in New Zealand and this is what it says:

'If one makes a career out of a challenging sport it is also in the back of families' minds 'IT' could happen, but if you were told when Billy was born you will only have this boy for 25 years because he will die from motorcycle racing injuries, would you have denied the absolute pleasure he got from that?'

The answer is no.

I wrote your name in the sky, the winds blew it away
I wrote your name in the sand, the waves washed it away
I wrote your name in my heart and now it's here to stay.

So proud of Mummy's little soldier

Love you
Mum and Dad

MUSIC

ALIVE – Pearl Jam

TRIBUTE TO BILLY
BY HANNAH WRIGHT

You never said I'm leaving,
You never said goodbye,
You were gone before I knew it,
And I'll never know why

There's so many times I need you,
And so many times I cry,
If love alone could save you,
You never would have died

Tears are falling constantly,
My heart hurts every day,
I think about your goofy smile,
And memories here to stay

I know you are still with me,
Your love is within my heart,
Though life is no longer present,
Our souls will never part

One day I know we'll meet again,
But its so hard to wait till then,
You are my love, my friend, my light,
But for now its time to say goodnight

TRIBUTE TO BILLY

by Lex Curtis and Alex Isaac

THE COMMITTAL

MUSIC

Highway to Hell AC/DC

BILLY'S RACING ACHIEVEMENTS

Anglesey International 2011
Novice Formula 600 • Position 1st

MGP 2014 Newcomers
Position 1st • Time 59:04:731 • Ave. Speed: 114.955 mph • Fastest Lap 117.102 mph
Additional Trophies: The Aitcheson Trophy, The Duncan Muir + Val Conaty Trophy, The Wallace Cup

MGP 2014 Junior 600cc Race
Position 2nd • Time 01:17:39:412 • Ave. Speed 116.605 mph • Fastest Lap 119.062 mph
Additional Trophies: The GD Hanson Trophy, The York Trophy, The Alan Hampton Trophy, The Hogg Trophy

Tandragee 100 2015
Superbike Race 1
Position 10th • Time 16:00:165 • Ave. Speed 99.777 mph • Fastest Lap 100.798 mph
Supersport Race 3
Position 6th • Time 14:00:511 • Ave. Speed 91.093 mph • Fastest Lap 92.637 mph

Southern 100 2015
Ellen Vannin Fuel Senior Race
Position 8th • Time 17:14.119 • Ave. Speed 103.566 mph • Fastest Lap 105.125 mph
Radcliffe Butchers 600cc Race
Position 6th • Time 17:31.615 • Ave. Speed 101.843 mph • Fastest Lap 103.133 mph
S & S Motors 600cc Race
Position 7th • Time 17:19.241 • Ave. Speed 103.056 • Fastest Lap 105.194
Manx Gas Solo Championship Race
Position 8th • Time 21:41.163 • Ave. Speed 105.828 • Fastest Lap 107.102
Additional Trophies: Best Newcomer in the Radcliffe Butchers 600cc Race, the S & S Motors 600cc Race, the Ellen Vannin Fuels Senior Race and the Manx Gas Solo Championship.

MGP 2015 Junior 600
Position 1st • Time 57:45.277 - Ave. Speed 117.591 mph • Fastest Lap 119.219 mph
Additional Trophies: The Tommy Club (120.028 mph) The York Trophy, J.W Davie Club Team Trophy

Bob Smith Spring Cup Olivers Mount 2016
Race 8
Position 5th • Time 1:59:567 • Ave. Speed 71.298 mph • Fastest Lap 73.164 mph

What manner of men are these who wear the maroon red beret?

"What manner of men are these who wear the maroon red beret? They are firstly all volunteers, and are then toughened by hard physical training. As a result they have that infectious optimism and that offensive eagerness which comes from physical well-being. They have jumped from the air and by doing so have conquered fear. Their duty lies in the van of the battle: they are proud of this honour and have never failed in any task. They have the highest standards in all things, whether it be skill in battle or smartness in the execution of all peace time duties. They have shown themselves to be as tenacious and determined in defence as they are courageous in attack. They are, in fact, men apart - every man an Emperor."

Field Marshal The Viscount Montgomery

DONATIONS

There is a collection plate located at the entrance to the Chapel, alternatively cheques should be made payable to Eric Faragher Ltd and then sent to:
Eric Faragher Ltd, 6 Main Road, Onchan, Isle of Man, IM3 1AS.
Donations will go to The Billy Redmayne Memorial Fund.

THE BILLY REDMAYNE MEMORIAL FUND

It is hoped to establish a charity called The Billy Redmayne Memorial Fund. The intention would be to use the Fund to support the needs of the Motorcycle Racing community with an emphasis on helping those up and coming riders who show great potential, but who are struggling to raise the finances necessary to move forward. The Fund would also be used to support the crucial work of the Air Ambulance Service. Although planning for the Fund is in its early stages we want to create a Fund which honours Billy. It would stand as a lasting tribute to him and his inspirational determination to win. Your help would be greatly appreciated and would ensure that the Fund can become a reality.

THANK YOU

Hannah Wright and The Redmayne Family

Please join us afterwards at The Villa Marina on The Promenade
(Postcode: IM1 2HJ) for a Party to celebrate Billy's life.

06/02/91 - 19/04/16

The next few pages are from the memory box we had at the Villa Marina where Billy's after party was held.

Remember when

You lost your phone on the piss and Lex felt bad so smashed his up. Then you found yours!

Hahahaha

Love always,

Bex

xx.

Silly Billy

Mr Billy

TT 2015

Will never forget the lap
In the 206 Billy & Rhys
arguing over the racing line
whilst me & Hannah didnt
dare look up sat in the
back, that week was the
best time I spent with
you Bill

Love you mate
GIBBO x

BILLY. ONLY BLOKE I
KNOW TO DO A GRAND SLAM!

RIP AIRBORNE

A PLEASURE TO HAVE KNOWN YOU!

LEWY

Billy R.

MESS IN

'D'

MESS

Turd!  A.

Do you Remember when
we...... CRASHed AT 90MPH!!
INTO A MANX STONEWall and
wrote OFF your mums
CAR with Nikki and the
police let you off Because
you were OFF TO AFGHAN
IN. A COUPLE OF DAYS & had
your para SHIRT on

I. DO :)

Billy you ARE CRAZY!!
FLY HIGH
MATE x

Kerry's face when
Billy Surprised her
by being at her
30th BIRTHDAY

x

• When we both came through the ranks of schoolboy motocross together.

Proud to of raced with you and to of known you Billy.

keep it pinned up there

Will Harrison

Myke Paxton xx
Daz Mac xx
RIDERS STAIRWAY TO HEAVEN!
RIP AIRBORNE

He believed in
himself and his
memory will live
on. Ride free

Keith & Di

x

13th May 2016

My Memory is a little 7yr old
boy who shared his bedroom
with a little boy from Wales.
They played together and later
raced together became firm friends.
Loosing Billy has devastated his
mate Rhys and Ben & Maria
Hardisty. We are privillaged
to have known him though!

Billy was very very Silli and Funny!

Catrin

Billy was always a
huge Support to the
Bell family + We all
loved him loads.
Hollie Mae has a huge
Crush on him but its
a secret.

XX

The Bells

- Our dads being work buddies!
- Watching you at the Boxing day Wanganui Races at the cemetery circuit in New Zealand 2014.
- And the old MX days!

You were so much fun, proud to have known you.

Love always Bills

xx Amy kneale xx

Will never forget holding your
hand Sue, when Billy first started
racing. He lived life in the fast
lane, and was a total credit to
you and Dave. I will always
remember the early days. You
are always in my heart and we
cannot forget the memories

Love Christine & Brian.

Hold your breath champion!

During 2014 AFGHAN tour we built a Swimming pool out of an old water container. It was about 11 feet deep and 7 feet wide. Whenever there was free time it was pool time, always coming up with new silly games to pass the time. These included jumping into the pool of a falklift truck at full extention, exercises under the water, passing silly messages to each other while sat at the bottom of the pool and holding our breath while holding onto a 25kg kettlebell at the bottom. Billy took on this chalenge as he does with everything and became the new champion with a time around 2.15 (Pretty impresive). An absolutely lovely bloke who I always looked up too and will never forget, Sue and

Dave he was a credit to you. and you have given him an amazing send off

Joel

"If one has not given everything, one has given nothing" Georges Guynemer.

The words that the "Letts" from New Zealand sent still stick with me and we would not have denied him the pleasure he got, the same applies to the Parachute Regiment as much as I would have liked him to have a normal quieter less hectic life and possibly marriage and children.

I would not have had him any other way, he was just Bill, along with the words that Kerry was brave enough to read out also ring true, 'why should I be out of mind just because I am out of sight'. I probably surprise a lot of people because I talk about him all the time, casually dropping him into conversations and why not.

I have no idea when we left the crematorium or how we got to the Villa Marina, I do remember we had photographs of Billy on a screen and on walking in the big room upstairs seeing my two very dear friends from the running club at the bar, where else would they be, other than that the whole evening was a blur, oh how I wish I could watch a rerun of it.

A few days later Dave went down to pay for the rooms they gave us one for free as that much alcohol was drunk that it more than paid for the room. Cheers everyone.

Most people left on Saturday my mum included, 'Paul the hat' took my mum from the hotel to the boat and then from the port home for us one less thing to worry about, in all we would have been a mess without their help, again that was down to how much high regard the parachute regiment held Billy, they not only sorted digs for the lads, but a full military funeral and later a military head stone for him it completely

blew us away when we looked back at what had been done for us.
That's how we think the seed was sown for what we wanted to do in the future to keep Billy's. memory alive and help other people who unfortunately end up like we did, but without military input. Little did we know it would happen so soon on Saturday 14th May Billy's sparring partner Malachi Mitchel Thomas had been killed racing in Ireland at the Northwest 200 we could not believe it, he was only 21 they got on well together despite what the race face photo showed. It is such a selfish sport. Dave and I thought it was only right to go to Malachi's funeral, so we did and met up with Hannah we stayed the night and came home. It was coming up to TT (Tourist Trophy) fortnight, I had decided I would try and go back to work after TT, bills still need paying and my ladies still needed looking after I did home care for the elderly and vulnerable. I just seemed to be so sad and low that I did not think it was fair to go back when my head wasn't right, there was also the fact that Billy should have been racing in the TT.
I didn't want him to do it, as I am more a fan of the Manx grand prix and southern 100 races, they seem to include the riders who are trying to get to the higher ranks out of the back of a van, but I suppose it's the ultimate race meeting, more so when you grew up here. I take my hat off to anybody who can finish the race, as that is an achievement.
Dave scrutineered the TT, I went up once but my heart wasn't in it, I went on my bike so I could make a quick getaway if needed, I went over to the Coffee stand whilst I waited for Dave, and realised it was Danielle and Conor Cummins mum Carol she gave me a big hug that meant more than words

could ever say, I finished my coffee got on my bike and left, not the right environment for me at that time. July arrived Dave and I were back at work as were the girls. The Southern 100 race meeting was happening now Dave was occupied at work and was a scrutineer at the meeting. I was thinking I should be doing more to help other families but was at a loss of what to do, work wasn't going to well I couldn't seem to function, and if one more person said to me 'life goes on' I would have hit them, no it doesn't, it might for you mate but not for me! I find you get up in a morning you try to function, you think about that person from morning till night, and if you can sleep, you dream about them, but they never answer your questions argh.

Dave and I booked to go to Armoy road races after the southern 100, Billy loved it there especially Acheson's leap, so I decided I was going to scatter Bills ashes there I had them ready in a little Tupperware dish.

So, Dave pulled in at the jump on the morning we were leaving, I got out of the van and said a few words and scattered him, then along came a waggon and the ashes blew back and hit me in the face, cheers Bill.

Billy at Acheson's leap 2015

September arrived and we were invited to The Gold Cup at Scarborough, I knew I had to do it for Billy's sake and mine, as I loved the racing at Oliver's Mount, whilst we were there, I am not sure which day, the police liaison officer came and had a chat with us, Hannah had come up for the day as well. To be fair the only thing I remember about that meeting is stickering John McGuinness's motor home with a Billy Redmayne racing sticker.

The Gold Cup Scarborough September 2016

As a family we had discussed opening a shop I had come to realise that I needed to look forward to something, be it something little like a night out or a weekend off island, with a shop it would be different every day we wanted it to be a unique kind of place, where you made donations for the food and drinks that you had, I also wanted to have books and a chillout place where you didn't have to be in a rush to leave, Kerry had always fancied running a book shop but with a play area for kiddies, Leanne wanted a 'proper' coffee shop, we decided along with Hannah what we were going to do, first of all where was it to be, we all agreed on Ramsey we also wanted it to be wheel and push chair friendly so the seed was sown could we combine it all together to keep Billy's memory and what he had achieved in his short life going.

We would try, now to find the right premises and make our wishes come true. I had done homecare in Ramsey and realised it had a lack of outdoor eating places and very few had wheelchair or pram access.

July turned into August and my first birthday without him I tried to focus on the fundraiser the girls were organising but couldn't, the Manx Grand Prix was fast approaching I was a shamble's. I did try to help but couldn't, so I kept away and let the girls sort it, they did a fantastic job of what I remember. I just turned up and drank too much but I also met a lovely lady whom Hannah had said was a small business lady, so I expected a small lady, but Helen was not small, she was tall, but she did help us later with the shop and is now known as" Helen the small business lady". The fundraiser made quite a lot of money to kick start the Billy Redmayne memorial fund, I will always remember our friend Kerry (Hooby) who now ran the Bridge pub in Laxey which sponsored Billy, turning up late and bidding for a collage of Billy's racing photos paying over the odds for it, whether Gail his wife forgave him for bidding under the influence I don't know. It now hangs in the Queens hotel in Laxey. Cheers Hooby Greaves we never tire of looking at it when we come to Laxey for a pint.

With the fundraiser now all done we decided to focus on looking for suitable premises in Ramsey, we looked at quite a few before we found the perfect one. The one we went for had an outdoor space, 2 floors a loo a kitchen and a mezzanine section perfect. Now time for the rent and paperwork to be sorted, but I now had a reason to get up in the morning something to focus on, don't get me wrong there were days I couldn't do anything except wander around crying, or taking the dogs for a walk finding somewhere secluded to sit and cry and scream. We signed the lease on October 1st, 2016.

We then got a phone call from a friend of Billy's who was ex para who offered us his family villa in Spain whenever we wanted a break, fantastic what a lovely gesture from someone we had never met. We decided to ask my brother Neil and his wife Helen and children Catrin and Ben, as they had been absolute rocks for us. We went in October half term with Neil being a teacher. We had an absolute ball, it had a pool and bars shops etc nearby, plus the weather was good, just what we needed, Ben was only 10 and upset at Billy's accident more so because Billy and Hannah had stayed at their house in the March, so it was raw for both children.

We came back to the news that the inquest into his accident was to be held at the end of November, great but at least it was this year and not being dragged into next year. Prior to that we had an invite by the parachute regiment to Billy's camp in Saint Athan for the remembrance service it was heart breaking but nice to lay a wreath and remember others who are no longer here and see all his mates and chat to other families who understood what it was like have lost someone. Next it was the inquest as usual I cannot remember much about it; I do know we stayed in a village pub in Brompton as the inquest was being held in Northallerton. Hannah met us at the pub along with Padre Jonathon. We had been advised to get a barrister, Helen my sister-in-law knew of a very good one through her line of work. All we wanted as a family was the truth, we could not believe that he had not seen a red flag, especially with his line of work! crash yes hit from behind yes but not stop for a red flag no. Apparently the marshals had left their post at this stage, so no wonder he didn't see a red flag. We do not blame anyone other than the clerk of the course for his accident, we all know the risks, but safety is paramount, and it was unsafe, an empty first aid base, which is why the race was red flagged 3 times. A rider needed morphine; the medical centre had none! the race was stopped so the ambulance could move around the track. Our barrister pushed and pushed the clerk of the course and asked the question "had the medical centre been correctly stocked the race would not have been red flagged and Mr Redmayne's accident could have been avoided". The clerk of the course replied yes. He never offered his condolences or even looked at us during the entire time, other riders that were involved in his crash did like Steve Mercer and Mark Gooding's .We spoke to the paramedic who was first on scene for Billy he was a lovely man, I asked him the question we all wanted to know the answer to, as a rider we all have a f--- s--- moment would Billy have had that, he assured me it was all too quick , that made me feel better. He also said if we thought of anything at all later to ring him, before we left, I asked what had happened straight after his accident, he replied they kept him alive until he got to Scarborough hospital and from there, he was airlifted to Middlesbourgh, these are the things you need to know as a family. Another nice genuine person that went above and beyond their job.

Hannah had done a lot behind the scenes to try and make it a safer circuit, we heard that Ivan Linton had lost the top of his finger at one race meeting and had to drive himself to hospital! And the way Hannah was treated after Bills accident was dreadful, no family liaison officer on hand for her and relying on someone you have only just met that day to help you is not acceptable, shortly after Billy's death in September 17, 12 spectators were injured in 2 separate crashes both riders were fine but 2 spectators were seriously injured and one lost a leg, Oliver's Mount in Scarborough was closed. It reopened in July 2019.

Time moved on slowly, Hannah had got tickets for sports personality of the year at Birmingham NEC, Billy and Malachi were getting a mention in the IN MEMORIAM section so we decided we would go and see what it was all about, it was quite surreal mixing with the sporting celebrities, like having Ellie Simpson stood next to me washing her hands in the ladies and Andy Murray's mum saying hello, I didn't know who it was until Dave told me.

Then Dave's claim to fame was using the urinal next to Gary Lineker oh, Andy Murray won SPOTY. It was upsetting seeing all the pictures on the big screen of those who had died in that year. After a good evening rubbing shoulders with the elite, we headed back to the hotel said our byes to Hannah and headed for a night cap, only to be sat next to the brilliant triathlete Brownlee brothers who were rather tipsy.

We headed home the next morning I knew we had a lot to do at the shop, which in a good way made me have something to focus on instead of the shitty black hole in my life. A few of Billy's friends came to the shop most weekends and we managed to get the entire inside of the shop painted it looked completely different. Now we had to start paying the rent it was very expensive to say it was on a side street not on the high street, but that's what we wanted just to pop up out of nowhere, we had set ourselves a date of the nearest Saturday to the 6th of February as that was Billy's 26th birthday so Saturday 11th it was. I think it was around this time we got a letter from a man that was the recipient of some of Billy's organs, saying a big thank you as he can now ride a push bike and play football with his children it was heart-warming and I could hear Billy saying, there you go mum pay it forward, there no good to me.

Christmas came and went, we were used to not having Billy at home for Christmas, but it still hurt as I knew he wasn't coming home in the new year. We did enjoy seeing little Evie Roses face with her presents and it was nice being together as a family the year before we weren't as we were in New Zealand; I can't remember if we went out for a meal at Christmas or New Year, but I know we had a good time Hannah came over so it was probably the new year.

Dave, Me and Evie Rose

To be honest I think the dogs got me through most of the dark days, they needed me to look after them and walk them, so I had to get out of bed each day. I was still having bad moments one day in the supermarket I had to leave my shopping and go and sit in the van, I had picked up a packet of Hollands steak and kidney puddings, Billy always had them when he came home, it just hit me from nowhere full-on sobbing with my head in the freezer dam it always happens when you least expect it.

We are now in 2017 and this is where things got tough, with myself and Hannah, we argued and screamed at each other it was very difficult for both of us as we both loved him so much, she had things of Billys that I thought as his mum I should have and Hannah thought she should have, the main ones being his dog tag and phone. We got through it though, but it was hard going for both of us.

It was around this time I think that we decided to empty his room and sort his things out, but to be fare a lot of his things came back from camp after his funeral in a big black box that the army call a comfort box, so we didn't really have a lot to sort out. We gave teddys and little bits to Evie rose and Leo. Some of his clothes to Rhys as they were roughly the same size. Ben my nephew got Billys collection of knives, better look after them Ben Wilkinson. Friends Justine and Jess who run JJ Ribbons in Laxey made me an outfit for brown ted out of Billys lucky socks and tee shirt, along with a cushion in Billys race colours and his logo and poppies on awesome. We gave Leo's dad Nikki a cigarette lighter and some other bits, the rest of his clothes we saved and had teddy bears made for the grandchildren out of them, by Ruby Roo keepsakes in Sulby, with love from Uncle Billy written on the buttons. I must confess I still have 2 boxes of his thing that I can't part with, and brown Ted shares our bed.

Cushion and Brown Ted's Outfit by JJ Ribbons

We now have 6 weeks to sort the shop and it's all hands-on deck, Dave coming after work putting light fittings up, Billy Cummins painted the outside of the shop for free, Splinters and Felton's (hardware stores in Ramsey) gave us a lot of discounts on the numerous tins of paint and many items of crockery that we needed. We got most of our furniture from the local amenity site and I upcycled them, all done as cheap

as we could. Next, we had to think of a name, I came up with Bilbos as that's what we called him when he was little, plus he wasn't here to disagree!
We ordered stock from random places mainly one-off items; I wanted the shop to be unique and sell quirky items. So one evening Kerry and I sat down and ordered a lot of Billy's merchandise, hoodies, tees, all in different sizes and colours, to be fair we did order far too much but, I think in my mind it was bringing him close to me, something that he had sat down and designed with Steve cooper (Zhoodz) and Hannah just before the race season, grief comes out in strange ways, but I did feel closer to him.

The café part and Leanne's Conrods coffee machine was now fitted by Connor himself and he also showed me how to use it, well he tried bless him patience of a saint. Billy's merchandise all on display around the shop, the top floor mezzanine / chillout bit had Billy's trophy cabinet thank you to Jamie Williams, he carried it upstairs for me, we put random photos of Billy up and dedicated it as Bills Bit, it had a TV and a settee to sit back and watch bike DVDs, and a stereo so you could listen to music. The first floor was arts and crafts, with upcycled tables and chairs 2 big comfy armchairs and a "ball pit" for toddlers to play and parents to chill. The ground floor was wheelchair/pram friendly thanks to Andy Fenton who made us a "singing dancing ramp" for free it made it much more accessible for people with mobility issues, including a lovely young man I met called Sean, he lived around the corner and came in most days in the end he became our wheelchair bound maintenance man, from sit down gardening to painting the resident bunny's cage, we are still friends now. We had a cosy fire upcycled fire surround and 2 comfy chairs surrounded by tables and chairs it was looking like a café, we had memorabilia and pictures on the walls we were good to go. The opening day came 10 minutes before the press and speaker (Jim Hunter) arrived Hannah went the loo and got stuck, the lock had jammed the window, it was tiny so she couldn't get through it, Dave managed to pass her a screwdriver and she unscrewed the lock, the electricity kept tripping out talk about dramas. The shop was ready, I wanted to do him proud.

The opening went well lots of people turned up I was very proud of what we had achieved but also apprehensive as we had never done anything like this before. Once we were up and running, I asked some of the customers if they knew of any people who would volunteer to help in the shop, a few got back to me and I ended up with the lovely Natasha and Pauline who helped out 2 days a week I had the fantastic Tommy on a Saturday but had to pay him, well he was a 13year old lad, and I had Sara when she was free, Carol the super cake maker, she made cakes for us every week sometimes twice, and not forgetting Rachel who was my go to in emergencies always ready to help out with just a phone call and a HELP and Dot price from the farmers market who every Saturday at 3pm dropped fresh vegetables and produce for us to get donations for, it worked well. I met lots of people and made some new friends ranging from the vintage motorcycle club to mums and tots.

It was around this time we learnt that Hannah and Billys mates had done a go fund me page and managed to get Billys bike from 2014 back for Dave, which was a lovely gesture. Dave did the parade lap in the TT on it then she came into the shop and had pride of place.

Exciting times

The Bike

I can remember Brad Vickers who the BRMF was sponsoring popping in with James Cowton I have never laughed so much they were both very witty and sarcastic a bit like a double act.

Mr Vickers

We had a busy TT despite the weather, friends from New Zealand Flea and Julie Willacy came over to see us which was a nice surprise they also wanted to promote the Tri Series out in New Zealand racing over 3 circuit's Tapo, Manfeild and the last one being in our friend's hometown of Wanganui on Boxing Day.

We held are fundraiser in August and sponsored Rhys Hardisty, Jamie Williams Brad Vickers and Jonathan Perry. It was held at the Villa Marina with Billys trusty Honda there as well and it was a huge success.

Fundraiser at the Villa Marina

We ran the shop for just under 3years, then decided not to renew the lease, the rent was crippling us, and the landlord would not reduce it. Also, we had now moved house and living in Ramsey, I wanted to be home more and spend weekends with Dave and the family. In November we booked a holiday to New Zealand Billy had loved it out there, so it seemed right to take him with us. Dave and I decided we would go back at Christmas, obviously as the bike racing was on and to scatter some of Billy's ashes after the racing.

We had a brilliant time swimming in the sea on Christmas day, watching motorbike racing then after the racing we went to do the ashes, well what a laugh it was quite windy, but his ashes just stayed on the start line, Flea said a few words and we waited and waited but they never moved, bizarre. We got invited to BBQs and had a fantastic Christmas dinner in Julie and flea's garden and met up with Boris from the Isle of Man's southern 100 club, he had flown over a few weeks prior to watch the cricket, it was a sad day remembering Billy but was also an enjoyable day with special friends.

#billyredmaynesticker Bay of Islands NZ

Cemetery Circuit Start line.

2018.

I think I would rather skip most of the chapter on 2018 as In May we lost Dan Kneen at the TT, July James Cowton at the Sothern 100 and Ivan Lintin seriously injured. We had decided to move house at this point, which was exciting but sad leaving all the memories, but we needed to move as the garden was not grandchild friendly with a river at the bottom, and you take your memories with you. Hannah had been in touch she had met someone from New Zealand Shane Richardson, it was lovely of her to let us know and apparently Billy had met him too. Then a few weeks later I had a someone run in the back of my new van whilst I was stationary, and I had to spend the night in hospital. One month later someone ran into the front of Bills car whilst the van was in the garage being mended, then just to cap it all someone ran into the side of my new mended van and did the front passenger wing in, you couldn't bloody write it and I must add not one was my fault. So not a good year, apart from the BRMF funded riders, James Field who got a third in the 600, Michael Rees 1st in the newcomers B on a 650, unfortunately James Smith broke down and Tom Robinson who was injured at the Southern 100 but very kindly returned his sponsorship money.

Michael Rees#28, Me and Dave, Kerry, James Field#14, Leanne and James Smith#29

Moving on to 2019

2019. As I have mentioned earlier I have to have something to look forward to, I am not so bad now in 2022, but in 2019 I could feel myself slipping again, I had been in a car accident in 2018 and had a fear of riding my bike I guess I felt vulnerable, if someone can hit me in a big white van, what chance have I on a motor bike ? I was also suffering from pain in my hip from the accident so I couldn't run either. In February we decided to book a week in Ibiza in April, the 3rd anniversary was fast approaching so to have a bit of sunshine and a chillout to lift me would be good, we had a great time and came back to the news our friends from Australia were coming for the TT Races at the end of May, we hadn't seen them since Billy had died. We had a wonderful catch and shared memories of Billy. Then amid what I thought was going to be a crap hard year, we got a letter inviting us the Memorial Arboretum in Stafford on the 19th of June and to Arnhem in September Eek were going to be busy of course we said yes and had a brilliant time such a peaceful and moving place with memorials for the military, police, air raid wardens to pigeons and everyone involved in the wars. Next, we had the Southern 100 races that Dave is chief scrutineer for, so he had a busy few days, we also have the 100 100 100, which is 100 laps of the TT course by 100 riders in a 100 hours, that takes some organising by Dave and Steve

We have a bit of respite before the Manx Grand-Prix in August and the BRMF fundraiser. In September we had been invited by the parachute regiment to go to Arnhem for the 75th anniversary. I didn't have time to feel down, my year was planned. This year for the for the Grand Prix the BRMF had sponsored Mike Brew who came 7th, Spanish rider Victor Ortega 9th, Dave Brook got a 6th, and Liam Chalk crashed at Kerromoar and had to retire with a hand injury. Despite the hideous weather and the change in the race programme making history, by the senior MGP race not being on Friday it was to be held on the Thursday. Well done lads, it was a fun filled night.

Victor Ortega #1, Liam Chawke #4, Mike Brew #5 and Dave Brook #17.

Me in Amsterdam

Once all the bike racing finished, we had Arnhem to look forward to we also had a couple of nights booked in Amsterdam.
A busy few months ahead which is what I needed. I had also decided to write a book about Billy and his amazing but short life, how I hadn't a clue. We also had the shop to empty, and I needed a job. Arnhem was a nice break after a hectic few month, whilst traveling there with the Army we met a couple whom we enjoyed many a night in the bar with John and

Moira Adams, they had lost their son Kyle whilst serving with 1 Para along with 2 other soldiers in Afghanistan, the Jackal they were in was hit by an explosion and small arms fire, he was only 21 what a waste of young lives.
The friends we have made in the army are like another family to us, the same as the biking family just a loss to a different sport. We are lucky in some respect as we have three different families we can grieve, and share are sadness and loss with.

Re-enactment of the drop at Arnhem

The Arnhem event was very moving from watching 97-year-old former Para Sandy Courtman do his tandem jump with the Red Devils, to the march on the bridge and the cemetery at Oosterbeek, throughout the service the local children stood quietly, ready to lay flowers on all the individual war graves, which is something that they have done since 1947 very moving. We decided we would go and have a walk and find the famous Pegasus Hotel I was glad we did as we met Billy's friends who announced us as "Wild Bill's Parents" and bought us quite a few drinks. Happy memories and I will go back one day.

We arrived home I managed to sort most of the shop out we were handing the keys over at the end of October, whilst sorting the shop I went to Teare's the local Butchers for some meat and left with a job, win win. The next event in this hectic year for us was the arrival of our daughter Leanne and Stevens little boy Joseph Billy, our first grandson born October 6thperfect and gorgeous. I had started work at the butchers that month as well, to my amazement I enjoyed it. November arrived and we met up with john and Moira at the Remembrance service in St Athan, that was a nice catch up. Christmas came and went; it was nice, but I've never been one for Christmas in the last twenty odd years bah humbug.
January 2020, we welcomed my Princess Evie Roses little brother Charlie to the clan once again gorgeous and perfect.
February came Billys birthday his 29th, it was also our friend Maria Hardisty's 60th so Dave and I decided to go over for her party in Abergavenny and catch up with friends and call in at Lancashire to see family, we unfortunately got stuck in Lancashire at Dave's sisters due to storms Dennis and Ciara as no boats were sailing. When we did get back little did, we know we had both got covid, we were both ill and in bed for 3 days, tired aching no appetite and a cough, it was only later did we realise that we must have caught it whilst away.

March brought Covid 19 to the island and we went into lockdown with the borders being shut to everything and everyone apart from keyworkers and freight. Dave worked from home, but my job was classed as essential, so I had my PPE and went in to work and did deliveries round the north of the island almost every day. As we all know it was a strange time, but we were lucky and got through it, I don't think it was as bad for us apart from no bike racing, but we were lucky enough to have the beach so close plus I could go for a run up to Bills bench at the Goose neck, or a jog around the Hairpin, and our children and grandchildren were here. Having two lockdown babies was hard more so on the girls especially Kerry as she also had to home school Evie Rose, Kerry and Martin were due to get married but obviously that was all up in the air but come June all was good they were to be married on the 10th of July in Douglas. It was a lovely day weather wise and nice to have something to be happy about after lockdowns , she looked absolutely stunning as did Leanne and Evie Rose, it was touched with sadness as well Billy would have been so proud that his sisters could scrub up well, at the meal it was strange as there was just one empty chair despite them knowing the amount of people in the small party, brought a tear to our eyes. Another event without him but we got through together.

The rest of the summer was spent walking and enjoying the sunshine, still it was strange having no Manx GP, but we survived just, I ventured out on my Ducati a few times confidence restored. We also went out to the pub more than we should, but it was nice after not being able to do, I often thought what Bills opinion would have been on Covid, one of his mates from the Paras called it "hat flu" for them that know

I thought it was good. Then before we knew it Christmas was here again, we had everyone round including Adam his partner and little boy George we were lucky.

2021

We entered 2021 quite upbeat we were able to go out on New Year's Eve for a few drinks, the family all came round on New Year's Day. Kerry and Martin were moving house next month lots to look forward to, then bang covid strikes again we were in lock down from 3rd January for 29 days. On Saturday 6th February we were meeting up with Billys friends to celebrate what would have been his 30th birthday, we had a meal and a good reminisce. It is one thing I do get sad at is the fact they are married now or have children that hurts that we will never have that, but hey ho. Kerry and Martin managed to move house successfully. Then it was announced no TT to risky which was true, so we had BBQs in the garden with family. At the beginning of July, we got an invite from the army to go to Colchester for the presentation of the new regimental colours, so of course we went it was quite scary on the underground it was so quiet and airports empty.

Prince Charles and Sir John Lorimer

We were met off the train by Billys friend Chris he was our host for the day, it was lovely to see him again he had just had another baby, so he got the obligatory BRMF baby tee. We were escorted to a tent and given a covid test then escorted to our seats not too far away from prince Charles it was quite an event. Later we went to have drinks in the marquee where we were introduced by the lovely Laura (parachute regiment liaison officer) to Sir John and Lady Lorimer, Sir John is the colonel in chief to Prince Charles, and they were moving to the island later in the year to be the queen's representative

on the island, what a lovely down to earth couple. It also turned out that Sir John presented Billy with the Fishmongers award. We spent a night in Colchester then back home, to organise a big BBQ for Dave's 60th where Dave stated he was not cooking, we had nice weather which was good, the grandchildren and friend's children had slides paddling pools out, and Steven and Martin cooked while Dave chilled, we had more than 50 people not including children he had a great day. In August it was my Birthday and our 30th wedding anniversary, which was pearl yuk, I was trying to figure out how we could celebrate it without too much expense when once again the army invited us to London, this time for Remembrance weekend, mm I could meet a pearly queen, and also go to St Athan Remembrance Day and feel close to my little soldier. We had organised a zip wire for Dave's birthday in Wales so we could do that and have a catch up with my brother and family, so we decided to do it all together, it took some organising with invites to our friend Marie Hardisty to stay a couple of night there to save driving into London. So first the Zip World Velocity 2, then on to south Wales to Marie's for a big feed and a bed. The next morning a train and hotel in London, also for my photo with a Pearly Queen, lunch at the famous Churchill Arms, an anniversary present from the girls, then a shopping trip on Portobello Road. We walked to the Fishmongers Hall on Tower bridge what an absolute gorgeous building and to think our Billy went in there and sat with some very important people, it did me good to see where he rang me from asking to borrow some money. The following day it was a remembrance service at the St Lawrence Jewry Church, another lovely building, we met some other parents who had sadly lost children but as

I've mentioned before, it's a family we all know what it feels like and could talk, cry, laugh together. After a lovely busy day, it was back on the train where Marie was meeting us, we went for a meal with Rhys and Becky a nice catch up. The next day was remembrance Sunday, so we went up to St Athan to Llantwit Major to pay our respects and drink in the pub that Billy loved. Then the following morning we were leaving to meet some of Bill's mates and padre Jonathon in the Green Dragon hotel in Hereford, but before we left Ian had some shocks off Bill's bike that he wanted Andy Grimshaw on the island to look at , so yes of course we will put them in the van and take them back, Ian had given them to Rhys who handed them to Dave in a General Purpose Machine Gun case we freaked out thinking we would get stopped by the customs on the ferry, we put them under my shopping bags and hoped for the best, I mean we didn't have a machine gun, despite what it said on the box. So off we went to Hereford such a lovely place, and the hotel was brilliant, we met Ian, Padre and another friend who had just come back from being involved with the terrorist attack in Liverpool. It was hard to think just ordinary men with families doing things like that for the safety of us and our country. We owe them much respect, anyway we had a nice meal and lots of laughs mainly at my son's expense. Then we left for Harrogate where our foster son Adam was meeting us, we had a night booked there before sailing back home, we had a good catch up with him and told him he was welcome to stay with us at Christmas with George, crikey where had this year gone. Once again Christmas came and went, very busy at the butchers luckily as it was a distraction for me, I was still finding myself getting upset at little things, cards saying merry Christmas son, or a

bottle of Hendricks Gin would have me in tears. There should be an island for people to go to who don't like Christmas, don't get me wrong I love it for the grandchildren, but obviously I get all melancholy sometimes. This year we were being responsible adults and were having Evie Rose and Charlie overnight on New Year's Eve as mum and dad were having a party. Rock and roll us.

2022

The year began on a good note, lots to look forward to, just what I need we had Billys birthday get together in February which always seems to arrive too quick after Christmas, a night out with his mates and their partners. We always have a "remember when" I find something new out each time. Then along came March rather quick to, we were looking forward to visiting friends that lived in Estonia, we had been invited to Sarah's 60th birthday, the war in the Ukraine had just started and although it was quite a way from where we were going there was still a bit of apprehension, but we all decided we would go I'm so glad we did we met the other half of the Brew family and it's a beautiful place. We also wanted to go to Joey Dunlop's memorial, which we did Billy idolised him, so we scattered some of his ashes there and placed a billy racing sticker very emotional.

Joey's Memorial

All to soon we were back home and back to work, Billys anniversary was coming up we always celebrate the day he died but this was a quite one compared to the past! whether that was because Bill's mate Joey was getting married and all the girls were away on Alex's hen party, I don't know. TT was approaching and we had friends coming over we knew most of them as they had been coming since 1998, but not every year. Good friends of our Rhys Hardisty and Becky were due there first baby in May so I knew Becky and baby wouldn't be coming, but still, I always look forward to seeing Rhys and his mum Maria. I worked during practice and race week but with only working part time I got to see most of what I wanted, and

went out most evenings with Mr Dickinson and co. We had an invite from Sir John and Lady Lorimer to attend the annual garden party at government house, of course we would go we also invited an amazing friend through biking to come with us, Mr Bjarne Johansen from Denmark, he had a great time and lots of photos. We later decided we would have the usual TT BBQ and invited all our friends that were over, Hannah and Shane where over, as I had never met Shane it was the perfect opportunity they brought their daughter little Maddie with them, who got on very well with our grandchildren it was brilliant to watch them together, but I won't deny it bloody hurt as well. The Aussies arrived by tram in the pouring rain only person to not show was Mr Allen Dickinson, but ill forgive him. But you couldn't write it, it absolutely poured down so it was held indoors luckily, we had enough room it was quite mad with four children running around, Dave and Wendy Heyes who now run Olivers Mount race circuit at Scarborough popped in which was nice as I had emailed a lot with her but not met either of them, they had been in touch regarding a memorial lap happening for Billy at Olivers Mount for the Steve Henshaw cup so we had a chat about that, which was nice to remember Billy .

All eerie and quiet now the racing is over, no listening to the bikes from the garden round the hairpin, waterworks and up to the Gooseneck, but I still enjoy living here when it's nice and quiet. Next up was the 100 100 100 laps that Dave runs with Steve Marsh usually falls around, 6th of July till 10th, its 100 laps of the TT course by 100 riders over 100 hours we usually start and finish at the Victory café on the mountain or the grandstand. It takes a lot of time and planning but it's

worth it for the charities we supported, this year its BRMF, Schoolboys MotoX and the Manx grand prix supporters club.

Sir John, Dave and Steve at the Joey memorial for the 100/100/100

Next up is the Southern 100 road races I much prefer this to the TT; it is known as the friendly races no airs or graces it's just all out the back of a van it starts on the 11th of July and finishes on Thursday 14th with a street party/awards presentation evening its brilliant and hardly ever any trouble. It was another brilliant event ran perfectly. Marie, Rhys and Becky were over for the racing as usual, and I got to see the gorgeous Nia adapting to life in the paddock like a natural at only a few weeks old.

I know I said I like to have things to look forward to, well it's been none stop since TT and we then receive a letter from the army asking if we would like to go to the national memorial Arboretum in Staffordshire in 2weeks time, well yes as I love going there it makes you realise you're not as alone as you think, we have met lots of families who have lost young lads in wars, it's such a peaceful place no matter how busy it is. We decided to see if we could get tickets for Hannah to come, which we did, Dave and I booked into a pub in the village 10 mins away, but as Hannah lived not far away, she was driving up. I had previously said to Dave that even though Billys name wasn't on the memorial wall I wanted some of him there, so I decided I would take some ashes and some for Hannah I placed them in a sealed bag in another draw string pouch and left them in my knicker drawer so I wouldn't forget him, we were packing to go a few days later I went to get my underwear out and the whole drawer was covered in sandy gritty stuff, it wasn't there this morning ? I shook everything and put it in the wash, I had been looking after the grandchildren aged 3 but the boys hadn't been upstairs, plus they couldn't reach, Evie rose had been at school , I was cleaning the drawer and that's when I spotted the pouch with the bag of ashes in, but the bag was inside and still sealed I freaked out and ran down stairs to show Dave, what the hell, to this day how Bills ashes ended up in his mums Knicker drawer remains a mystery.

The Ashes

(That bits for you Laura McPhilemy) We had a lovely day with Hannah meeting new faces and catching up with old. Hannah scattered some of Bill's ashes, it was nice for her to have somewhere near home, rather than Isle of Man or Scarborough.

Dave and I had one more night in Stafford before home and a rest before the next round of racing in August. My birthday came and went 14th August, omg 60 next year, grand prix arrived along with friends of ours from Accrington who were staying for a few days. Then as quick as it arrived it was almost over; the lads went home prior to our fundraiser cheers boys like we didn't need your help. We were holding the fund raiser at the brilliant Mitre hotel in Ramsey it coincided with Ramsey rocks which is bands playing in the street, Karl had let us have the room for free, despite it being one of the busiest nights for him. He is a star, we got in early to set up but only Dave and I were free at that time as the girls had their families to see to before coming. I was in total panic I hadn't heard from the wonderful Stuart Perks who was the entertainment for the next few hours, we had tables chairs, merchandise and food to sort. The next thing I know is a man and lady in bike gear are carrying merchandise into the room chatting to Dave, she sorted all the tees and hoodies out for me whilst her hubby helped Dave with the heavy stuff, I thought Dave knew them, it turns out they were parked behind the van and offered to help unload it! We got chatting and invited them to the fund raiser, we'll be rude not to. Rachael, Matt, Dominic and Aaron arrived early thankfully, as they helped and entertained the riders for us while we warmed the food cheers Carl.

Kelly #54, Paul #29, Albert #31 and Gareth #38

The fund raiser was a success our riders did us proud we had sponsored Gareth Arnold, Paul Cassidy Albert Walker and Kelly Carruthers all were good value and were brilliant with the children, as was the hilarious Dominic Herbertson who was our guest speaker, it was like a double act with him and the fantastic Chris Kinley they had everyone laughing.

Stuart Perks the Entertainer

Chris Kinley and Dom Herbertson

Stuart Perks was awesome singing and playing the guitar, it's down to people like you that keep the newcomers going, with helping raise funds for next year to all of you a big thanks.

October arrived it was nice to have a quite time, well as quite as we can get. Andy Fenton a friend of ours from the racing scene had taken over the responsibility of looking after Billys bench, at the gooseneck for us, and near the end of October the bench had gone? in June end of TT we had someone remove a small tree in a large pot, never to be returned, but no someone wouldn't pinch a bench? Then Andy rang he had removed it, powder coated it and assured us it would be back for remembrance, and it was so we walked up to the gooseneck me Dave and the dogs and had a toast to all the fallen, then into Ramsey to lay our wreath, then out, out.

Pistol Pete, Dicko, Clay and Beau with us at Billys bench at the Gooseneck

Then before we knew it, we are in December and we had all been invited to the organ donors service in Douglas, Diane Taylor who has become a friend of ours, joined the organ donors committee after her son Daniel was killed in a car accident in in January 2007 aged the family donated his organs. Billy was friends with Daniele through moto x and was shook up to say the least when the accident happened, I always remember Daniels cheeky smile. Diane then went on to be an organ donor ambassador for the national health blood and transplant team in the UK. It's through Diane that we heard about the organ donors memorial garden at Nobles hospital it was set up in 2015 and we now have a stone there for Billy which the grandchildren enjoy going to, less daunting than the crematorium. Evie Rose loves going to Billy's Garden, and she was brave girl at the memorial service, she got up and lit a candle for Uncle Billy. The service itself is wonderful with screens showing all the people on the island who have donated organs, but it's not done in a sad way, it still doesn't seem real to me when I see Billy up there but it's a nice way for the grandchildren to remember him. It's now the week before Christmas, were both busy at work and looking forward to a few days away over Christmas, but I still did the usual elf in the ashes before we left to keep Billy company.

We have booked a cottage in Derbyshire and taking the dogs with us, it will be hard being away from the grandchildren, but they had all there present's so they wouldn't miss us.

Dave and I had a nice, chilled time walking eating and drinking. We came home in time for new year and luckily Leanne hadn't had my 3rd grandchild despite a few scares. We had all the family round including foster son Adam and his son George the kids had a sandpit that we bought them we set it up in the conservatory for them, it was chaotic but wonderful, despite the empty chair. Freddy made his entrance on January 12th, much to the delight of his big brothers Jack and Joe. February Billys 32nd birthday arrives, we have our usual night out with the boys and their partners, I asked how long are we doing this for? they said forever.

Then we had Mr Martin Brunnschwieler ring and asked us for a logo and a name for a beer he was launching for the governor Sir John Lorimer, he also wanted to include Billy as he was a para, like Sir John, with a 20p per pint going to BRMF, we were all overwhelmed Billy would have loved it. Martin wanted to launch it at the Beer festival on the 6th of April and wanted us as a family to pull the first pint with Sir John, we have known Martin since we moved to the island over 30 years ago, he also sponsored Billy's racing.

Just to make are lives a little bit more hectic we had decided to have a web site set up for the BRMF, Happy Dog Images put us in touch with Brian from The Advertiser Online, who was brilliant we couldn't have asked for a better website, I love it we launched it at the end of March. Here we are now on 7th April the beer festival was last night and was a success the beer is lovely I think we liked it, maybe Dave and I liked it a little too much. When I set out to write about Billys life warts and all, I knew I wanted to finish it in April basically where it started, so today is the day. This month for our getaway in April we are going a week after his anniversary we are going to Exmouth for the Falklands Cup, it is a football match between the Parachute Regiment and the Marines, we are also hoping to catch up with the wonderful padre Mr Jonathon Daniel and his wife.

So here we are in the month I hate, it changed me and my life forever I'm just not the same as I used to be. What should have been the start of a fantastic race season for Billy turned into my worst nightmare. Most people expect you to move on in time, you carry on but don't move on as you don't want to, you want to remember. Some of the hardest things I found was people avoiding you, in supermarkets or crossing the road it was like they thought they could catch death off you, people you thought were friends and whom you used to have a drink with not getting in touch or calling like they used to do. It's weird like after a few months like you should be over IT. Then, you have the families of riders who have died getting in touch via face book, like the family of Gavin Lupton who died of similar injuries to Billy I have never met Jacqui his mum or Jessica his sister, but we all share the same hurt. When I think of the riders who have died, they have one thing in common its usually the eyes and the dark humour, but the one thing we all have is we are in the same shitty club. Things that probably won't change and still give me a "Moment" are sell by dates yep, especially from 17th – 19 April, I always say mmm Billy was definitely better before then and have a moment.

Billys favourite food or drink on tv, supermarket or restaurant can set me off. Music I still get flash backs as to where I was, relating to Billy and hearing a certain track. Smells still now certain smells take me back to places I don't want to be like the hospital. Hospitals definitely give me a moment, seeing someone on tv in a hospital gown, or on life support. Last the empty chair always gets me!

Some words that I can relate to, but I have no idea where I saw them, Grief it never ends but it changes, it's a passage not a place to stay Grief is the price of love that we pay.
Richard E Grant said, "I don't think you get over grief, but you go round it, it's a daily navigation". Very true
Sometimes I feel sad that I have missed out, on his children and I get sad when I see mums and sons of his age, or someone moans about their son, I always think at least he's still here! but on the other hand I am so proud of him and what he achieved and experienced I can honestly say hand on heart I would rather have Billy do what he did for 25 years and have no regrets than he live to be 30, 40 or 50 wishing he HAD done something.

You live more for 5 minutes going fast on a bike than other people do in all of their life. "Marco Simoncelli"

One thing I don't think I will know the answer too is, why when something doesn't physically hit you, you hurt so much like you have been kicked hard in the stomach and it only eases every now and then?
The years have passed but the memories stay, we miss you still every passing day you brought us pride and lots laughter your smile will remain for ever after.

Moving on into the future we will continue to raise money for Billys memorial fund, our daughter Kerry has said she will continue when Dave and I can't. At present I am looking forward to my 60th birthday with doing a lap at Greg Lamberts sidecar school as a passenger in a sidecar if my arthritis lets me, it’s something I have wanted to do since I was 17. I even wrote to Jim will Fix it (glad he didn’t fix it for me). I am also hoping to go up in a chinook helicopter, if possible, all to raise money for the BRMF.

I WROTE YOUR NAME IN THE SKY, THE WINDS BLEW IT AWAY
I WROTE YOUR NAME IN THE SAND, THE WAVES WASHED IT AWAY
I WROTE YOUR NAME IN MY HEART AND NOW ITS HERE TO STAY.
BILLY X

THE END

30046213 LANCE CORPORAL
BILLY T REDMAYNE
THE PARACHUTE REGIMENT
19TH APRIL 2016 · AGE 25
BILLY. A LIFE WELL LIVED
UTRINQUE PARATUS
GUINNESS
GUINNESS

Now for some stories and tributes about Billy

On the 4th of January I left the Isle of Man to go travelling. I was meeting my friend in Cairns Australia.

Billy was already in Afghanistan on his first tour at this point. Mum was planning on running each day he was gone. This put my mind at ease a little as I knew she would be kept busy and occupied whilst we both went about living our dreams. As this was what the tour was to the mental case that is my brother, to go on tour and do what I would call the scary stuff! But to him it was what he had been training for.

The hard thing was keeping in touch with him. I couldn't talk to him from my mobile when he tried to call, this was due to me being all over the place I think and not in one place for long enough. However, we talked over Facebook messenger about what we were each up to. Well, mainly me telling him, as his stuff was top secret!!

Once I left Australia at the end of February I went to New Zealand, for the month of March, they had the best burgers ever in Queenstown - the Fergburger, this was soon to become a firm family fave as Billy, Leanne, Mum & Dad were soon to discover how amazing these burgers are when Billy raced over there in 2015! Hannah and Mark had had them before on previous trips.

My travels took me to Asia where I still wasn't able to talk to Billy, but we remained in touch over messenger sharing my travel adventures and telling him he needed to go to Thailand - to which he actually listened to me for once and went on holiday with the lads in 2013.

KERRY, BILLY'S SISTER

I remember Billy coming home from the hospital when he was born, I was 5 and Kerry was 7. From that day on Billy had 3 mums, much to his annoyance! Having 2 big sisters it was inheritable we would mother him, as he got older, he referred to us as mum 1, 2 and 3...and ever the loving brother, more often than not, greeted me as 'knobber' whenever we met up.

Over the years I saved Billy's arse on a few occasions! Occasionally alcohol was involved, and he became a bit of a hot head but he also had a tendency to choke when in my presence... The first time he was 4, I remember mum had him upside down hysterical whilst I hit him on his back to dislodge the sweet he was choking on, I had been going to first aid classes so put my new found skills into action!! Another time he went purple whilst choking on a piece of chicken...but a few hard whacks on the back and he was fine!

I remember him ringing me from Glasgow one night, he was on the piss with some of the lads, I was at Uni in York, early hours of the morning my phone rings and it's Billy. He's in a taxi going to A & E as he's been glassed in the face and has no money to pay for the taxi! Why he rang me as a skint student I have no idea but I'm glad he knew he could ring his big sister for help.

When Billy was motor cross racing, we would sacrifice our Sundays to be the supportive sisters and freeze our arses off in the wind & rain marshalling at Ballagaraghyn, West Kimmeragh or Knock Froy. One time Billy was practicing up at sky hill and me & mum went as driver and snack suppliers, he fell off, hurt his knee...as he rolled up his trouser leg his knee bone was visible, I'm sure, his knee had split open from one side to the other. I was trying to be all low key about it and reassure Billy it wasn't that bad, but we headed off to A & E to have it looked at, where I proceeded to faint while we were waiting to be seen! Ha-ha.

Although he was the 'baby' of the family Billy was also there for me a few times too, one occasion he piggy backed me all the way back to our campsite from the pub as we discovered I can't handle more than two pints of Kroonenberg!

We have so many memories growing up, camping holidays, going to Tenerife where he had his first alcoholic drink and got a bit tipsy with Dad, me babysitting him and sending him to the shop for sweets, which then turned into him sending me to get him and his mate's alcohol from the shop! Shooting targets with his air rifle in the garden at Ivy Dene, he was a good teacher.

I remember the last hug I got from Billy, it was when we were parting ways after spending two weeks in New Zealand together, along with Hannah, Mum & Dad. Billy was racing at Cemetery circuit in Wanganui on Boxing Day but before that we spent some time travelling around, playing frisbee golf, luging, beaching and generally having a blast in Queenstown, Wellington, and all the places in between. It was the best two weeks of my life up to that point. As Me, Mum and Dad were going on to Australia, Billy and Hannah were heading home, Billy gave me a big hug goodbye and I'll never forget that big hug. It wasn't the last time I saw Billy; he came over to the Isle of Man in March 2016 for a visit and we met in The Bridge pub in Laxey for a drink and a catch up, that was the last time I saw Billy before his accident.

I don't dwell on how Billy died and the awful time following; I try to remember the good times and laugh and share stories with friends and family.

Now I've got two boys of my own, Joe and Freddie, I tell them all about their uncle Billy and we look at photos of him racing and as a Para and generally just being 'Billy'. I'm so proud of Billy, to me he wasn't just a soldier and a racer, he was my big, little brother XXX

Leanne

Memories of Billy

Neil had asked Billy if he wanted to earn some cash and come and stay with him whilst he was renovating our old property, lucky for Neil he agreed and gained some muscles in the shape of Billy and another young local lad. Billy was a great help shifting tonnes of rubble and stone by hand, he stayed for a week, living in a tent in the derelict house, cooking on a camp stove and walking the 3 miles each way to the pub in the evening.

Billy, Kerry and Leanne all managed to coincide a visit to our house together in North Wales, after it had been renovated, which was great seeing them all together, Billy came up on his motorbike, much to the delight of Catrin and Ben, who weren't for letting Billy leave until they had sat on it several times, tried on his helmet and revved the engine! We all took the kids up to Llyn Brenig, the big lake by our house, and went on a walk and had a play in the woods. The adventure playground had never seen so many big kids, the biggest of which was Billy, who played with kids for ages, being silly and having fun. We finished it off with a hot chocolate and cake in the cafe.

Neil went to watch Billy play football at Tranmere for the Isle of Man against Tranmere Rovers academy with his mate Caerwyn. Billy's team came second!

When the kids were little, we frequently went over to the Isle of Man on holiday as the kids enjoyed spending time over there. The time often coincided with Billy being on leave and we have memories of the kids firing Billy's BB guns and him teaching them how to shoot it and walking the dogs. Catrin and Ben always loved seeing the dogs, and Ben had a real affinity for Nip, Billy's dog.

Before Billy went out to Afghanistan, we managed to help him out with his kit and bought him some boots to go out with, we also remember sending over a few parcels whilst he was there with a selection of sweets and chocolate and other entertainment in the form of magazines!!!

We had a few trips to watch Billy racing, in some form or other and have memories of going to Barrow in Furness to watch him race motor cross, with Catrin when she was 18 months old, and Ben hadn't been born. We took the kids up to Scarborough to see Billy race and they loved seeing him and sitting on his bike, not so much the noise of the racing, but they enjoyed being around him.

Billy came to stay in March 2016, the month before what was to be his last race. He came up with his girlfriend Hannah and we are both very grateful for these memories. We went to watch the Banff Mountain film festival and visited a few other touristy places in North Wales, including surf Snowdonia. We obviously made it out for a few drinks in Conwy where we met up with Dan one of Billy's mates from the paras and someone with whom we would regularly meet up with after Billy's death. Billy's love for dogs was more than apparent that evening in Conwy as he was far more interested in petting a local's dog than conversing with us! We wished him luck with his race and waved our last goodbyes.

It was early evening on April 16th, and I was ironing and had a phone call from Sue, she said Billy had been in an accident racing. I asked if I could do anything and she said no, 5 minutes later I spoke to her again and I before I knew it, I was in the car driving up to Scarborough.

Hannah and Lex were at Billy's beside when I arrived, and it was an overwhelming state of emotions realising the extent of his injuries. Sue called me or I called her, I can't quite remember but I distinctly remember her saying on the phone 'tickle his toes', or it could have been 'pinch a toe' and that would wake him up, I obviously did this knowing it wouldn't change anything, but Sue needed me to try.

It seemed to take forever before Sue, Dave, Kerry and Leanne arrived at the hospital, I remember watching them walk past the door of the waiting room I was sitting in with other people who had arrived, I put my head in my hands as I knew what they were walking in to. I remember having time on and off with Sue and telling her she could get through this and trying to console her and the family, but words were fruitless.

The time at the hospital was filled with tears, anger, whiskey, emotions, and people, lots of people arriving which was a credit to Billy and the young man he was. I don't think the Intensive Care Unit has seen so many people crammed into such a small space to say their goodbyes.

The following day was strange, and we spent time with Billys mates, some of whom we had never met before, it was great to hear stories of Billy and it was particularly amusing when we were talking about him over a pub lunch and one his mates' meals fell in his lap it was almost like Billy was having a few last laughs.

Uncle Neil & Auntie Helen

Billy … Where do I even begin? It is so hard to find the words to talk about our time together; whilst I love reliving our adventures, it's a painful reminder of what could have been. I will never do our story justice, but I hold all our memories so close to my heart. I met Billy in December 2013 at a charity event raising money for JJ's memorial fund. After a brief chat outside, Billy was so drunk that he ran into a revolving door. That memory always brings a smile to my face.

Billy and I spoke on social media for a while and in February 2014 I went to Cardiff to celebrate my friend Kate's birthday. Billy was there and after a few drinks, we finally plucked up the courage to talk to each other. He told me that he really liked me, but nothing could happen between us as he was going away for 6 months. We continued to text and then Billy told me that he didn't care that he was going away, and he came to visit me in Coventry a couple of weekends later. Billy asked me to be his girlfriend on the 19th April and our whirlwind adventure started there.

Billy then went away for a few months on tour, and I went and worked out in America at a summer camp. It was hard with the time difference, but we always made sure we had time to video call each other. During Billy's R and R, he was racing in the Manx Grand Prix. This was my first taste of road racing and I was hooked. I completely fell in love with the Isle of Man and me and Billy always talked about moving there one day. Billy had an amazing run at the Manx Grand Prix; he won the Newcomers race and came second in the Junior Race. I remember being at the gooseneck with Billy's mum Sue and his sisters Kerry and Leanne watching the newcomer's race. We were watching and listening to the radio and Kerry was trying to work out if he had won, when we realised that he had we all screamed and raced to get back to the paddock to see him. I was so proud; this was something that Billy had worked so hard for. It was such a strange feeling watching Billy race; I was in awe of how talented he was but also sick to my stomach with worry.

From then on, I went to every road race with Billy. He dubbed me his 'pit bitch'. We created some amazing memories, and I will treasure them forever. Tandragee was our first Irish Road Race and me and Becky nearly died sleeping in the van because of the Guinness farts! It was such a wet rainy weekend and I remember that Billy was on his bike waiting to go out. A lot of the riders had team members holding umbrellas for them, so I ran back to the van but all I had was a little purple umbrella with an owl pattern on it. I didn't want Billy to get wet, so the owl umbrella had to do. That photo made it on to the BBC website!

Armoy was Billy's favourite Irish Road Race. His friend Malley was spannering for him that weekend and I always remember that we wanted to watch the big bikes race from the jump section. Billy was convinced he knew how to get there, and he had us wading through cow fields and over barbed wire fences. When we finally got there, we realised there was a path that went pretty much direct to the paddock. Billy wouldn't admit that he was wrong though, he just wanted us to take the 'scenic route.'

Another memory was at the Northwest; Billy made his way to the grid and I walked down with his dad Dave and Becky. Once we were on the grid, I said to Billy, 'where's your helmet?'

He just looked at me with sheer panic. He had left it at the van, which of course was my fault, so I had to sprint back to get it. Becky had to sprint after me because the van was locked, and she had the keys. We were parked up in the furthest corner away; but I made it back just in time.

One night at the Northwest, me and Billy went for a walk looking out onto the beach and there was the most amazing sunset. It was nice for us to get away from all the craziness and spend some time just us. I remember looking at Billy and feeling completely content. Being in a relationship with a road racer had its difficulties; the weekends away, the time spent on the bike, chasing sponsorship but I wouldn't have changed it for the world. One race weekend at Oliver's Mount, Billy had booked us into a hotel as a treat as I had done my fair share of nights in the back of a van. We got back to the hotel after a day at the track and there was a box on the bed. It was a pandora charm for my bracelet that he had bought me, and it had the word 'dedication' written on it. He had bought it as a thank you for all the support that I gave him for his racing. It was such a nice feeling to know that I was appreciated.

In 2014 Billy was invited over to New Zealand to race in the Suzuki series and he went with Lex and Ash. The following year he was invited back, and I travelled over with him. His mum, dad, Leanne and family friend Eggy also came, as well as one of his friends Ringo. Billy rode for Biggles racing which was owned by Marcus Beagley. Helping on the spanners was a guy called Joel Dykstra who was recruited via Facebook, but who went on to become a good friend. We always had a good laugh at the track with the team, even when Billy blew an engine which meant a super late night.

As the racing happens over Christmas, me and Leanne tried to make our rental car more festive with tinsel. We watched the film 'The Holiday' on Christmas eve and then on Christmas morning we opened our presents. Billy bought me the most beautiful Pandora ring and a charm to go on the bracelet he bought me the year before. We then had a Christmas breakfast with Flea, Julie and Sam at their house which we all really enjoyed. Later that evening we went to Joe and Barb Letts house for Christmas dinner. It was so strange not having a traditional Christmas dinner, but it really was amazing, and we were so thankful that we were made to feel so welcome. Our time in New Zealand was incredible, we did so much travelling around and we both fell in love with the place. We spent so much time in the car, but those drives were awesome. The scenery was beautiful, and we would just blast our music with not a care in the world.

Me and Billy also went on holiday to Egypt in November 2014. We spent most of our time drinking in the sun and it was just perfect. On one of the days, I made Billy come on a couple's spa day with me. We were taken into a wet room where there were two beds, and we had a full body scrub then we were hosed down. We laughed from start to finish. Particularly when they took us through for a massage and made us hold hands. We were giggling away like school children. I think Billy secretly enjoyed it though.

Away from racing, me and Billy spent as much time together as we could. He would travel to Coventry, and I would spend time on camp with him. When I went to visit him on camp, we would always end up in one of the pubs in Llantwit Major. We always had such a good laugh, usually followed by a horrific hangover and fry up at Coast the next day.

Billy moved in with me and my mum in February 2016 and we bought our first house shortly after. We were so excited to be taking that next step in our lives. We had so much to look forward to; everything was falling into place. Billy was going to be riding the MV provided by Jack Valentine with the support of Des and Dot Collins, as well as riding his own bike. We had worked so hard renovating his beloved ambulance so life at the track was a little more comfortable. Billy was set to debut at the TT, and he was so excited. Although everything was moving in the right direction for us, it wasn't always perfect. Our relationship could be fiery at times; we both had tempers and Billy could be a stubborn pain in the arse, but I was so lucky that I got to see a side to him that not many people saw. Billy could be super affectionate, and he would always tell me that he loved me. He was so protective of me, and he always pushed me to be my best. Not only was Billy my boyfriend, but he was also my best friend.

Billy and I always talked about our future; we had picked names for our kids and planned on getting married. On New Year's Eve following our time in New Zealand, we were at my auntie and uncles house and Billy had a few drinks and let slip that he knew what engagement ring he was going to buy me, and he knew where he was going to propose. I had a feeling that it was going to be on the same walk at the Northwest with the beautiful sunset; we were planning on going there again the following May. I never did get to find out what his plans were. There are so many more things that I could talk about, but I would be here forever because we crammed so much into our two years together. We always said that we lived life in the fast lane. Billy was one of the most incredible people that I have ever met, and I am so lucky that he chose me to create a future with. Although that didn't happen, we spent two years completely and utterly in love, and for that, I will always be grateful.

HANNAH BILLYS PARTNER

Billy.

I've many fond memories of which i will cherish forever. Most of our conversations would revolve around the same stuff, bikes and racing, profanity insults & ill humour mainly.
me and Billy first met when we met the whole of the Redmayne clan for the first time when my late father was competing at the TT in 98. We were welcomed into their home on a home stay, it was brilliant and the whole family where welcoming helpful and generally ace. I think it safe to say they became lifelong friends and more from this point on, extended family as far as I am concerned. The whole family helped us through a tough time that would change are lives' for ever...all be it on the whole for the worse but without doubt a big plus point was the family bond that was made. I will never forget what they did for me and mam and am forever in their debt. Especially Dave, on that particular day on which he held my hand dried my face and took a young,

frightened lad and made him a man to take on the bad news to come. I believe this action and character of the man is exactly what crafted the man that Billy became without doubt.

Me and Billy were bunked up as young pups, Leanne and Kerry where in the attic... and if I remember the world cup was on and Bill at this age was football mad. After this point, I wasn't to see Billy or the Redmayne family for many years, contact was kept through Christmas cards and emails and so on. Thanks mum! with regular updates on Bill's mx antics, and off to be a soldier. I'm sure there's many a story of this part of his life from the lads he served with. Many of which I've heard and enjoyed from some of them, and from Billy. When we met again.

We'd been messaging and in contact again which was great to catch up, Bill had been away serving and, on a trip, back home, the doorbell rang and there stood the man. ambo parked up in street the lot. this is where it all picked up it was like we'd never lost contact. Instantly it turned to racing and Manx Grand Prix in particular. Billy was going the 600 A newcomer option I was going 650 B newcomer route. we were both hell bent on winning. he did!! my race was cut short after DNF at Crosby on first lap. I was gutted...obviously, especially as we were on track to win it, I believe. To have both bikes on podium that had been prepped and run out of Dave's garage in Laxey would have been the dream! I sat on the bank and listened to the race on a marshal's radio, I knew Billy would be up for it... the man was a machine. before we made our way to the start line he was in back of ambo with Creedence Clearwater

Revival's, Fortunate Son on the CD chain smoking Marlborough cigarette's, he was shaking and wound up like a clock, in a good way...he was like a kid that had seen a pair of tits in a jazz mag for the first time... he didn't go to the line to race...he went to the line for war, and failure wasn't an option. I knew before it even started it was his, it was his destiny. he referred to Bray hill as the closest thing adrenaline wise as going into gunfire. He lived for it.

We later hatched a plan to go to Ireland and see some real road racing, the whole thing was bloody brilliant, from Guinness farts to hangovers lying in a wet muddy paddock taking the awning down in aim to catch the boat back sleeping 5/6 up in the LDV pissing in bottles not to have to walk to the toilet block at North West200 as they hid our van as it wasn't catching on the eye, to having to pressure wash the van to get it in paddock, from wins at Tandragee and a shit run at NW200 we had a ball.

One particular stand out memory was playing silly buggers after his Junior win in 2015 and my Classic TT podium, we were playing street luge in shopping trollies down Douglas Highstreet, despite his broken ribs hahaha that was funny, crashing all over the place Becky and Hannah going mad!! Pissed up fun.

On coming around the mountain for the last time I saw a black figure going nutts with the marshals jumping up and down...at Graham Memorial he was giving me hand signals all race...I knew it was Bill and he'd broken down, when I saw him jumping up and down like a looney on final lap I thought I must be going all right then.. something I will never forget.

Billy was infectious in more ways than one, his confidence made you confident. He wanted to be successful, he also wanted you to succeed, the qualities of the man were endless.
Scarborough.
Billy hated the place from our first trip there...
The second trip wasn't much better. Bill took the ambo, so was set up by time we got there.
after an off and all the toys being thrown, he calmed down I said we could get the bike back out if he wanted to run on Sunday, eventually he agreed he got out and got a decent finish. he said he would never go back.
We all know what happened after.
Everybody lost something special that day.
I didn't lose a Soldier, a brother, partner ...
I lost a Real Friend, someone who understood me, helped me and so much more.
The confidence Billy had was incredible, the talent, skill & drive he had were not plagued by a big ego, he was the real deal.
No bull shit, No full factory wanker, he was a man on a mission.
He was a turd, a goon, a thunderc*nt a bloody liability when he'd had a few ...but most of all he was a bloody fantastic Human. A really fast one.

RHYS HARDISTY

"I'd heard of Bill long before I met him. I rode motorbikes for a blood bike charity and considered myself to be pretty quick.
When Bill and his cohort joined the rifle company, I was the medic for, I knew I'd have to go for a bit of a blast with him.

Eventually we met, and a ride out was discussed. So, on an overcast Saturday me and Bill rolled out of the camp gates and on to the roads of South Wales. As it turned out, the first road we found ourselves on was a firm favourite for both of us. It's a really quick flowing series of bends with short kinks to change direction between farmers field boundaries. It's mainly flat apart from one small dip, immediately followed by a super short climb that table tops. It's also got a slight bend in it. Usually when I approach this table top, I lean in to the turn, roll off the gas a little, crest, front wheel still lifts then settles and away you go.

On this day, we covered the distance to the table top fairly briskly and where I would usually start to roll off, I witnessed the first sign that Bill was anything other than a normal rider. He took a much narrower line than I would, hunched forward, threw his elbows up into the air and quite literally pinned the throttle.

The result was a CBR 600 now clearly, and by quite some height, airborne over this crest.
I'd never seen anyone do that before. And have not seen anyone do it since.

For the next hour I made a brave effort to stay with Bill as we punched up through the south Wales' valleys and into the Brecon Beacons. We stopped for some lunch, and I confessed that I was surprised at how aggressively he went into corners. He just shrugged and smiled. I was aware that Bill was ultra-competitive. I'd heard about him on the ranges with a rifle, he was a fucker for trying to beat the other lads either with speed or accuracy.

Alas, lunch finished so we jumped back onto the bikes, and I balked at the weather which in typical Welsh style was now starting to piss down. Proper Welsh rain. Any hill became a sheet of travelling water, any flat became a pond.
Now I was on a Daytona 675 with wet weather tires on. I'm more than comfortable riding in the wet, in fact, I really enjoy it.
And if I'm being completely honest, I was quite smug as I expected that this would probably slow 'wild Bill' down a tad as he had dry track day biased tires on.

Imagine my surprise, nah, imagine my horror, when instead of slowing down. This bloke sped up, the same tell-tale elbows high in the area, dropping the bike into the corner on a positive throttle, through the apex, hard on to the gas again and he'd exit like a bullet.
You have to ride smooth in the rain. But here was Bill charging about, making sharp changes in direction, hard on to wet brakes, harder onto a squirming rear tyre.
On a pristine wet track it would be ballsy, entertaining riding. On this less than perfect climb out of Neath into the black mountains it was nothing short of maniacal.
Never did he get more than 60ft away, never did I get closer than 20ft.... whilst I imagine his heart rate never lifted above

60bpm, I don't think mine ever came below 120....

At the end of the day, we rolled on to camp and I admitted I was expecting him to ease off in the wet.
' nah, i love riding in the wet, you can get more of a slide coming out the corners... plus other guys don't like riding in the rain so if I can ride quickly in the wet I can potentially take points from them in racing'

Well quite.

I don't recall actually getting to ride with Bill very often after that, we did a track day which was as expected. Ridiculously fun, and fast. But I can't seem to remember actually riding on the roads with him again.
I watched him race at Aintree whilst he was trying to earn enough points to get into road racing...
what I witnessed during our road ride was amplified when he was racing on track. For context, he was on an older, former road registered bike, it had less power and normal road brakes when compared to the majority of the people he was racing against. Yet come the end of the long straight at Aintree, he'd be the last on the brakes, fish tailing as the weight of the bike started to lift at the rear and the back wheel lost traction, the bike would settle and he'd throw it hard into the right hand sweeping corner, elbows up, and he'd be building pressure on the throttle until the front was getting really really light, as the corner straightened he'd pin the throttle, the front would lift before he was completely upright and he'd shimmy onto the next straight. It was pure exhilaration to watch him race. He wouldn't win these earlier races, not because of a lack of talent, he was racing on a

soldier's wage. Against guys that had professional backing and sponsorship. That he finished the races at all sometimes was impressive, that he finished amongst the top in his field consistently is almost beyond belief." **RINGO**

Billy was out in either Swansea or Cardiff and as usual missed the train so to save money on a taxi or hotel they would find some Biffa bins(nice ones) one story that printable is Billy and Lex finding some with card board in (not daft mum keeps me warm) Lex got into one, a while later Billy hears Lex saying mines better it's got a comfy pillow, next morning poor Lex his pillow was a dead cat! How p----d was he. One story that I have probably got a bit wrong is one that Lex read out at Billys funeral, they were out doing what they did in Afghanistan when Billy shouted out and fell on to the floor, Lex picked Billy up and carried him back to the compound shouting medic and put Billy on the floor to which Billy sat up and gave the finger and said it was just my sore knee you dick. **LEX**

R.I.P Billy

Every now and then you meet someone who makes a real difference in your life. In our sport that's something that seems to happen even more rarely. A sport that as much as we love it, all too often leaves us jaded and disillusioned. Billy was one of those rare people who made a difference.

Billy Redmayne was a breath of fresh air. He took us two "old hands" in Jack and I and reminded us why we love the sport. Despite his obvious talent he really was as green as the hills and in all truth that's one of the things I liked. A raw, untamed talent that wasn't tarnished by the bad sides of the sport. He rode for enjoyment, ambition and because he loved it. Just so happened that seemingly unknown to him, Billy was good. Very good.

Along with this raw talent came Billy himself. A fantastic, driven, warm, smart, and friendly young man that approached everything this new opportunity brought to him with a maturity most seasoned riders are unable to muster. His excitement for this new season was only equalled by his desire to do it right. Not just to rush in like so many do and waste it all through ego. Ego was something Billy had no time for.

As I got to know him, I grew increasingly proud of this young man and even more proud to be building him a bike for the TT. A serving Paratrooper in his daily life, that alone in my book makes him a hero. Added to that he reminded me why I do this job. He reminded me what I love about the sport

and reignited my enthusiasm by giving me a chance to help a rider who was set to be a front runner of the next generation. A rider who was so willing to learn and absorb everything you told him. A rider who people would want to look up to and was far more than a large percentage of the current crop of new riders who are little more than hair gel and a pair of expensive shades.
Billy was the real deal.

My heart goes out to Billy's family. He was a credit to them. At the very least they can take great heart in knowing just how many people thought so highly of Him. They can be truly proud of their son.
Then there's Hannah his girlfriend. Hannah was Billy's rock and the driving force behind so much of what made Billy great. The bravery and strength I've witnessed from her in the last few days has been awe inspiring. Billy would be so proud of you.

I'm truly honoured to of known Billy, even if it was for all too short a time. I can't explain how sad I am for what's happened. We've been robbed of one of racings future stars and a true friend.
Ride safe buddy. Someday I hope we meet again.

Dave Hopkinson

"An MV Agusta for his first TT" was the title originally given to the article about Billy Redmayne; this in itself was indicative of the progress Billy had made in his short time as a road racer. Alas, sadly, this as we know will not be the case as Billy tragically lost his life in an accident whilst racing in the Spring Cup at Oliver's Mount.

An immensely talented and probably the most exciting and promising Manx born motorcycle racer for several years, Billy was due to make his TT debut in 2016 having made a huge impact at the Manx Grand Prix during the last two years. During the early spring this year, Billy answered our questions in preparation for an article which would be an integral part of a theme in this issue, that of the Manx Grand Prix being a breeding ground for TT talent possibly more so now, than since the days of Hislop, Lougher and Dunlop.

Billy's answers were meticulous in detail, factually interesting and full of anecdotes; it was one of the easiest and most enjoyable articles to write.

Securing photographs was not a problem... all our normal contributors had action shots of Billy, not unsurprisingly at last year's Manx where his battles with Malachi Mitchell-Thomas will be talked about for years to come.

Billy's article was to have been five pages in length in the colour section towards the rear of the magazine and was to include six photos – five action, the other shown here, with him in a contemplative mood after pulling in at the approach to Braddan Bridge during practice last August with a blown engine on one of his Classic machines.

Billy's early experiences of racing revolved around moto cross, then, with the support of his family, he turned to the tarmac,

combining racing with life in the armed forces. In 2008, Billy had joined the British Army Parachute Regiment completing 3 six-month tours of Afghanistan in the last eight years: a Lance Corporal who won several prestigious awards, he felt this gave him a
unique strength, both physically and mentally and valuable life experiences to help with the huge challenges that a rider can face in pure road racing Billy sensationally won 2014 MGP Newcomers' A on a bike bought and proudly built by himself and his father on a shoestring budget... and this having only just qualified for his national licence the year before; later that week he finished a close second to Andy Lawson in the Junior race.

In 2015 he represented the Martin Bullock Full Factory Winnerswear team at the MGP, Southern 100 and Post TT meetings; he was also able to race in the Pre-TT Classic and Classic TT events on 750 and F2 Classic machinery provided by Team Collins and Russell. At the MGP, despite a fall in practice Billy
was able to renew his great duel with his sparring partner from 2014, Malachi Mitchell-Thomas. Pitting after his first lap in the Junior, he found that his practice crash was taking its toll on his performance though his shoulder and hand were ok, his painful cracked rib prevented him pushing on as hard as he would have liked; he had to back off, but not too much, being able to keep a slender lead in the end. He felt it was the most painful hour of his life but was rewarded for his great efforts by being able to celebrate another victory over the Mountain Course!

Billy retired in the Senior whilst in second place but did set a lap of 121mph… from a standing start! For this year's TT he was due to ride his own, Billy Redmayne Racing Kawasaki ZX10R, backed by thepeoplesbike.com along with Jack Valentine's Valmoto 675 MV Agusta backed by both 'Support our Paras', the Parachute Regiment's charity, and Des and Dot Collins. His aims were top 20 finishes on the big bike, pushing past the 126mph mark in so doing and positions as close as possible to the top 10 on the Supersport. Our sport has lost a fine young man, who knows what he could have achieved – his fledgling career had shown so much promise? Our condolences go to his partner,
Hannah, his family and all his many friends.
Sally Bly

The first time I met Billy was in 2008 after my extended post tour leave in Fiji upon returning from Iraq. I was so lucky to work closely with him from 2010 to 2014 during his 3 tours of Afghan. A very humble, competitive, and hard-working person.

We did a winter Afghan tour together in 2010-2011 and then we changed company as we got back to the UK just so we can have a summer tour. I remember vividly in 2014 when he came back from RnR and I have never seen him so happy. He told me that he has met a girl (Hannah) and he said that she is the one for her. I told her that it might just be the RnR blues (if there is such a thing), and he said I quote "T-Bag, no mate she is the one".

We went for CLM Course to Colchester and we shared a room with 2 single beds. On the Thursday night, we decided to explore the town as we were meeting with another guy from 2 PARA. As the night went on, the 2 PARA guy was having a fight with a SNCO from the garrison. We just looked at them and Billy said to me, "T-Bag look at those 2 idiots trying to ruin the night for us." We went back to the hotel and instead of going to bed, we manage to convince the night staff to open the bar for a few more drinks. It was in this drinks that we had a good conversation about what we wanted to do. For him, it was trying to get time off from the Unit so he can concentrate on racing, and he was going to drive up North as soon as we get back to STA for a race that he said he does not need to attend but need some cash boost for the big one (Isle of Man TT). I asked him why he cannot find another hobby compared to the motorcycle racing and he said "T-Bag, I'm from the Isle of Man and secondly I would rather die doing what I love and enjoy even if my body is all messed up instead of a body that just looks beautiful in a casket".

We went to bed as we were supposed to be in class at 0800 next day and obviously that did not happen. I woke up at about 1000 and when I looked over to his side of the room, he was staring at me. As soon as our eyeballs met (as we knew we are late for the lesson) we just gave each other smirks as we knew the consequences of our action. I then said to him, "What are they going to do about it but send us back to STA?" We laughed it off and went back to sleep waiting for the guys to get back from camp. About an hours later, Tim knocked on our door and as soon as we opened it, he barged into our room and said you bunch of idiots, I have to cover and make up an excuse for you 2 when they called out your names and I told them you were called back to camp as you were on CT.

Some stories about Billy which I will not be able to share on here that happen on operations due to its sensitivity and I ended up getting interrogated for it.

The good moments we shared together Billy has just become memories and those memories are the best things I have of you.

T-Bag (Tui).

Bill would regularly appear outside my door at ridiculous hours, absolutely shitfaced and dressed in nothing but his birthday suit, AB webbing and of course a PARA REG Beret.

He would then bang furiously on my door and insist on me opening up for him to come inside and "chat" or another favourite he would use was that "something was going on and needed help".

Every time it was convincing enough that I cracked the door ajar to see if it was "GEN". Obviously, it was utter bollocks, and he would then boot the door open and multiple blokes would come barging in. Their weapon of choice for most "insertions" were likely to be FIRE EXTINGUISHERS from our block or "acquired" from another block.

Being gassed and drenched in fire extinguishers in your own room at 3am by a group of highly intoxicated and very naked PARATROOPERS, has to be one of the most gopping things to happen to myself and many more unfortunate souls whilst residing in BLOCK 103.

Revenge was sweet the next morning. As Bill slept soundly in his bed and no doubt suffering a hideous hangover from last night's antics, I snuck into his unlocked room (CROWBAG MISTAKE) and filmed with great pleasure, the terror in his face as I gassed him in his pit! That video is still priceless even now.

Cheers Bill, it was a pleasure!

Dan

There are so many stories of us all growing up together, but these are a few of my favourite memories with Billy.

When we were in high school, we usually stayed at Dave and Sue's at the weekends, there was a time when me and Billy were smoking at the bottom of the garden and heard Sue come home so we panicked and I ended up falling in the river!

I had never been on a bike before and Billy decided to let me have a go on his 85, did not end well because I lost control and ended up in a bush - Dave and Billy couldn't stop laughing and took the piss out of me the rest of the day. 😂

Whenever Billy was home on leave we would go out and usually end up in Havana on the dance floor with jugs of Purple Rain or bottles of wine/champagne.

We were all out one night and got into a fight and Nikki ended up being arrested - me and Billy were walking through town after and he was fuming so he tried to kick the window at Boots but it was raining so his foot just slipped up the window and he ended up on the floor, we were both laughing our heads off.

On another night we were sat in the pub playing spoof and Max lost the game, so he had to take a dirty shot. He downed it but brought it straight back up and Billy was not letting the shot go to waste, so he got a straw and sucked it up. 😂

We were lucky to have him as our best mate, there's not a day that goes by that we don't talk about him and all the mad stuff we got up to!

Joey

We all met Billy in year 7, we never got along at first and laughed when he tripped and split his eyebrow open whilst being cocky playing football at school. Fast forward a year or so and the madness begins. We all start to get along. Obviously, the years and years of stories could fill a book but here's a few shorts from over the years.

Back in the early days we would be constantly waiting for Billy whilst he was sorting his barcode fringe out whether that be in a pane of glass or car wing-mirror. Sometimes we would be a good way down the road and he would still be at it even if we were running for a bus.

We would find absolutely anywhere to chill and drink our beer. We once found our way into a house that we thought was abandoned in hindsight it wasn't abandoned, full electrics, heating. Etc. All came to an end when Billy pissed down the wall right over a socket and blew the electrics. All he did was laugh and giggle whilst finishing his piss.

We would often stay at Billy's because we would get the last bus home so get to stay out later, giving us time to try and finish our cans of beer - although the struggle was real when we hit Laxey's Wheel Hill. Often ending up collapsing on the bank halfway up. Remember waking up, having breakfast, and then helping Billy with his chores. That was the only downside. Or Dave would be taking us out in the motocross bikes.

Remember being in Quid's Inn once and we ended up arguing with a couple of people and either got kicked out or went outside for smoke and these individuals start gobbing at Billy through the window. He casually punches the window in and tells them to get outside! Safe to say they bottled it.

Billy would often show up at my house, banging on the door or window at 5am whilst on leave. Even though I hadn't answered his 20 calls prior. Leaving me with no choice, but to have a beer or two and listen to him waffle mad shit to me then fall asleep an hour later.

Nikki

A big thank you to all who helped me to write this book. Especially Dave when it got tough, and bloody hell it did get tough.

Sue

All proceeds from this book will go to The Billy Redmayne Memorial Fund. For more information, please visit us at our website. www.billyredmaynememorialfund.co.uk

Thanks to Baylon McCaughey for the front cover photo.

Printed in Great Britain
by Amazon

36562230R00126